MY BLACK HORSE

NEW & SELECTED POEMS

Tess Gallagher

BLOODAXE BOOKS

ISBN: 1 85224 306 6

First published 1995 by
Bloodaxe Books Ltd,
P.O. Box 1SN,
Newcastle upon Tyne NE99 1SN.

Bloodaxe Books Ltd acknowledges
the financial assistance of Northern Arts.

Cover printing by J. Thomson Colour Printers Ltd, Glasgow.

Printed in Great Britain by
Cromwell Press Ltd, Broughton Gifford, Melksham, Wiltshire.

For my mother
GEORGIA MORRIS (QUIGLEY) BOND,
and for
RAYMOND CARVER

ACKNOWLEDGEMENTS

Acknowledgements and thanks are due to Tess Gallagher's American publisher Graywolf Press for poems selected from her collections *Instructions to the Double* (1976), *Under Stars* (1978) and *Willingly* (1984), as well as from *Amplitude: New and Selected Poems* (1987) and *Moon Crossing Bridge* (1992). Her introductory memoir *My Father's Love Letters* is reprinted from her book of essays *A Concert of Tenses* (University of Michigan Press, 1986).

Acknowledgements are due to the editors of the following publications in which some of the previously uncollected new poems first appeared: *American Poetry Review, American Voice, The Honest Ulsterman, Kalliope, The Meaning of Life* (Time-Life Books, 1992), *Mirabella, New York Times, Parnassus, Passages North, Santa Barbara Review, Virginia Quarterly* and *Witness*.

Tess Gallagher wishes especially to give thanks to Greg Simon, who helped immeasurably as she worked on the new poems. She also gives thanks to the Lyndhurst Foundation for providing a grant which allowed time for writing. Thanks are also due to Dorothy Catlett, who contributed greatly in spirit and fact, and to Lawrence Gallagher for the cover photograph of Tess Gallagher on her horse Angel Foot taken on her grandfather's farm in Windyville, Missouri, in 1972.

CONTENTS

FROM **WILLINGLY** (1984)

FROM **AMPLITUDE** (1987)

MOON CROSSING BRIDGE (1992)

I.

II.

III.

Words lead to deeds ... They prepare
the soul, make it ready,
and move it to tenderness.

ST TERESA

MY FATHER'S LOVE LETTERS

It's two days before Christmas and I have checked myself into the Dewitt Ranch Motel. 'We don't ask questions here,' says the manager, handing me the key to number 66. I let him think what he thinks.

The room is what I need, what I've been imagining for the past two days – a place with much passing and no record. I feel guilty about spending the money, but I've trusted my instincts about what it will take to get this writing done. For the past week I've been absorbed with student manuscripts and term papers. At the finish, I discover I have all but vanished. Coming to the motel is a way to trick myself out of anonymity, to urge my identity to rise like cream to the top again.

I had known from the first moments of being asked to write about my influences as a writer that I would want to get back to the child in me. For to talk of influences for a writer is essentially to trace the development of a psychic and spiritual history, to go back to where it keeps starting as you think about it, as an invention of who you are becoming. The history which has left its deepest imprint on me has been an oral and actual history and so involves my willingness at a very personal level. It involves people no one will ever know again. People like the motel room I write this in, full of passing and no record. The 'no record' part is where I come in. I must try to interrupt their silence. Articulate it and so resurrect them so that homage can be paid.

To speak of influences, then, is not to say 'Here, try this,' only 'This happened and this is what I think of it at this moment of writing.'

I want to begin with rain. A closeness, a need for rain. It is the climate of my psyche and I would not fully have known this if I had not spent a year in Arizona, where it rained only three glorious times during my entire stay. I begin with rain also because it is a way of introducing my birthplace on the Olympic peninsula in Washington State, the town of Port Angeles. The rain forest is a few miles west. The rain is more violent and insistent there. Port Angeles lies along the strait of Juan de Fuca and behind the town are the Olympic Mountains. The Japanese current brings in warm air, striking the mountains, which are snow-covered into June.

It is a faithful rain. You feel it has some allegiance to the trees and the people, to the little harbor with its long arm of land which makes a band of calm for the fishing boats and for the rafts of logs soon to be herded to the mills. Inside or outside the wood-framed houses, the rain pervades the temperament of the people. It brings an ongoing thoughtfulness to their faces, a meditativeness that causes them to fall silent for long periods, to stand at their windows looking out at nothing in particular. The people don't mind getting wet. Galoshes, umbrellas – there isn't a market for them here. The people walk in the rain as within some spirit they wish not to offend with resistance. Most of them have not been to Arizona. They know the rain is a reason for not living where they live, but they live here anyway. They work hard in the logging camps, in the pulp mills and lumberyards. Everything has a wetness over it, glistening quietly as though it were still in the womb, waiting to be born.

Sudden Journey

Maybe I'm seven in the open field –
the straw-grass so high
only the top of my head makes a curve
of brown in the yellow. Rain then.
First a little. A few drops on my
wrist, the right wrist. More rain.
My shoulders, my chin. Until I'm looking up
to let my eyes take the bliss.
I open my face. Let the teeth show. I
pull my shirt down past the collar-bones.
I'm still a boy under my breast spots.
I can drink anywhere. The rain. My
skin shattering. Up suddenly, needing
to gulp, turning with my tongue, my arms out
running, running in the hard, cold plenitude
of all those who reach earth by falling.

Growing up here, I thought the moss-light that lived with us lived everywhere. It was a sleepy predawn light that muted the landscape and made the trees come close. I always went outside with my eyes wide, no need to shield them from sun bursts or the steady assault of skies I was to know later in El Paso or Tucson. The colors of green and gray are what bind me to the will to write poems.

Along with rain and a subdued quality of light, I have needed the nearness of water. I said once in an interview that if Napoleon had stolen his battle plans from the dreams of his sleeping men, then maybe I had stolen my poems from the gray presence of water.

The house I grew up in overlooks the eighteen-mile stretch of water between Canada and America at its far northwest reach. The freighters, tankers, tugs, and small fishing boats pass daily; and even at night a water star, the light on a mast, might mark a vessel's passage through the strait. My father was a longshoreman for many of these years and he knew the names of the ships and what they were carrying and where they came from: the *Kenyo Maru* (Japanese), the *Eastern Grace* (Liberian), the *Bright Hope* (Taiwanese), the *Brilliant Star* (Panamanian), the *Shoshei Maru* (Japanese) – pulp for paper, logs for plywood, lumber for California. He explained that *maru* was a word that meant that the ship would make its return home. I have been like these ships, always pointed on a course of return to this town and its waters.

On Saturdays my father would drive my mother and my three brothers and me into town to shop, and then to wait for him while he drank in what we called the 'beer joints'. We would sit for hours in the car, watching the townspeople pass. I noticed what they carried, how they walked, their gestures as they looked into the store windows. In other cars were women and families

14

waiting as we were, for men in taverns. In the life of a child, these periods of stillness in parked cars were small eternities. The only release or amusement was to see things, and to wonder about them. Since the making of images is for me perhaps 90 percent seeing and 10 percent word power, this car-seeing and the stillness it enforced contributed to a patience and a curiosity that heightened my ability to see. The things to be seen from a parked car were not spectacular, but they were what we had – and they promoted a fascination with the ordinary. My mother was an expert at this: 'See that little girl with the pigtails. I bet she's never had her hair cut. Look there, her father's taking her in there where the men get their hair cut.' And sure enough, the little girl would emerge twenty minutes later, eyes red from crying, one hand in her father's and the other clutching a small paper sack. 'The pigtails are in there.'

Every hour or so my mother would send me on a round of the taverns to try for a sighting of my father. I would peck on the windows and the barmaid would shake her head *no* or motion down the dim aisle of faces to where my father would be sitting on his stool, forgetting, forgetting us all for a while.

My father's drinking, and the quarrels he had with my mother because of it, terrorized my childhood. There is no other way to put it. And if coping with terror and anxiety are necessary to the psychic stamina of a poet, I had them in steady doses – just as inevitably as I had the rain. I learned that the world was not just, that any balance was temporary, that unreasonableness could descend at any minute, thrashing aside everything and everyone in its path.

Emotional and physical vulnerability was a constant. Yet the heart began to take shelter, to build understandings out of words. It seems that a poet is one who must be strong enough to live in the unprotected openness, yet not so strong that the heart enters what the Russian poet Akhmatova calls 'the icy calm of unloving'. Passion and forgiveness, emotional fortitude – these were the lessons of the heart I had no choice but to learn in my childhood. I wonder now what kept me from the calm of not loving. Perhaps it was the unspoken knowledge that love, my parents' love, through all was constant, though its blows could rake the quick of my being.

I was sixteen when I had my last lesson from the belt and my father's arm. I stood still in the yard, in full view of the neighbors. I looked steadily ahead, without tears or cries, as a tree must look while the saw bites in, then deepens to the core. I felt my spirit reach its full defiance. I stood somehow in the power of my womanhood that day and knew I had passed beyond humiliation. I felt my father's arm begin to know I had outleaped the pain. It came down harder. If pain could not find me, what then would enforce control and fear?

I say I entered my womanhood because I connect womanhood with a strong, enduring aspect of my being. I am aware, looking back, that women even more than children often serve a long apprenticeship to physically and psychically inflicted threat and pain. Perhaps because of this they learn more readily what the slave, the hostage, the prisoner, also know – the ultimate freedom of the spirit. They learn how unreasonable treatment and physical pain may be turned aside by an act of faith. This freedom of spirit is what has enabled poets down through the ages to record the courage and hopes of entire peoples even in times of oppression. That women have not had a larger share in the history of such poetry has always seemed a mystery to me, considering the wealth of spiritual power that suffering often brings when it does not kill or maim the spirit. I can only assume that words have been slow in coming to women because their days have, until recently, been given over so wholly to acts, to doing and caring for.

During these periods of travail I did not stop loving. It was our hurt not to have another way to settle these things. For my father and I had no language between us in those numb years of my changing. Through my attempts in the poems, I have needed to forge a language that would give these dead and living lives a way to speak. There was often the feeling that the language might come too late, might even do damage, might not be equal to the love. All these fears. Finally, no choice.

The images of these two primal figures, mother and father, condense now into a vision of my father's work-thickened hands, and my mother's back, turned in hopeless anger at the stove where she fixed eggs for my father in silence. My father gets up from the table, shows me the open palms of his hands. 'Threasie,' he says, 'get an education. Don't get hands like these.' Out of this moment and others like it I think I began to make a formula which translates roughly: words = more than physical power = freedom from enslavement to job-life = power to direct and make meaning in your life.

There were few examples of my parents' having used words to transcend the daily. The only example was perhaps my father's love letters. They were kept in a cedar chest at the foot of my bed. One day I came across them, under a heap of hand-embroidered pillowcases. There were other treasures there, like the deer horn used to call the hounds when my father had hunted as a young man. The letters were written on lined tablet paper with a yellow cast to it. Written with pencil in a consistently erratic hand, signed 'Les' for Leslie and punctuated with a brigade of XXXXXs. I would stare at these Xs, as though they contained some impenetrable clue as to why this man and woman had come together. The letters were mainly informational – he had worked here, was going there, had seen so-and-so, would be coming back to Missouri at such and such a time. But also there was humor, harmless jokes some workman had told him, and little teasings that only my mother could have interpreted.

My mother's side of the correspondence was missing, probably because my father had thrown her letters away or lost them during the Depression years when he crossed the country, riding the rails, working in the cotton fields, the oil fields, and coal mines. My mother's lost letters are as important to remember as those I'd found from my father. They were the now invisible lifeline that answered and provoked my father's heart-scrawl across the miles and days of their long courtship. I might easily have called this essay *My Mother's Love Letters*, for they would have represented the most articulate half of the correspondence, had they been saved. That they are now irrevocably lost, except to the imagination, moves them into the realm of speculation. The very fact that my mother had saved my father's love letters became a sign to me as a child that love *had* existed between my parents, no matter what acts and denials had come after.

16

As with my parents, invisible love has been an undercurrent in my poems, in the tone of them, perhaps. They have, when I can manage it, what Marianne Moore called iodine and what I call turpentine. A rawness of impulse, a sharpness, a tension, that complicates the emotion, that withholds even as it gives. This is a proclivity of being, the signature of a nature that had learned perhaps wrongheadedly that love too openly seen becomes somehow inauthentic, unrealized.

My father's love letters were then the only surviving record of my parents' courtship and, indeed, the only remnant of their early love, for they never showed affection for one another in front of us. On a fishing trip years after I'd left home, my father was to remark that they had written to each other for over ten years before they married in 1941.

My father's sleep was like the rain. It permeated the household. When he was home he seemed always to be sleeping. We saw him come home and we saw him leave. We saw him during the evening meal. The talk then was of the ILWU longshoremen's union and of the men he worked with. He worked hard. It could be said that he never missed a day's work. It was a fact I used in his defense when I thought my mother was too hard on him after a drinking bout.

Stanley Kunitz has seen the archetypal search for the father as a frequent driving force for some poets, his own father having committed suicide before his birth. It occurs to me that in my own case, the father was among the living dead, and this made my situation all the more urgent. It was as if I had set myself the task of waking him before it was too late. I seemed to need to tell him who he was for me, and that what was happening to him mattered, and was witnessed by at least one other. This is why he has been so much at the center of my best efforts in the poems.

The first poem I wrote that reached him was called 'Black Money', this image taken from the way shoveling sulfur at the pulp mills turned his money black. He had come to visit me in the Seattle apartment where I lived as a student and I remember telling him I'd written this poem for his birthday. I had typed it and sealed it into an envelope like a secret message. He seemed embarrassed, as if about to be left out of something. Then he tore the envelope open and unfolded the poem. He immediately handed it back to me. 'You read it to me,' he said. I read the poem to him and as I read I could feel the need in his listening. I had finally reached him. 'Now that's something,' he said when I'd finished. 'I'm going to show that to the boys down on the dock.'

Black Money

His lungs heaving all day in a sulphur mist,
then dusk, the lunch pail torn from him
before he reaches the house, his children
a cloud of swallows about him.
At the stove in the tumbled rooms, the wife,
her back the wall he fights most, and she
with no weapon but silence
and to keep him from the bed.

In their sleep the mill hums and turns
at the edge of water. Blue smoke
swells the night and they drift
from the graves they have made for each other,
float out from the open-mouthed sleep
of their children, past banks and businesses,
the used car lots, liquor store, the swings in the park.

The mill burns on, now a burst of cinders,
now whistles screaming down the bay, saws jagged
in half light. Then like a whip
the sun across the bed, windows high with mountains
and the sleepers fallen to pillows
as gulls fall, tilting
against their shadows on the log booms.
Again the trucks shudder the wood framed houses
passing to the mill. My father
snorts, splashes in the bathroom,
throws open our doors to cowboy music
on the radio, hearts are cheating,
somebody is alone, there's blood in Tulsa.
Out the back yard the night-shift men rattle
the gravel in the alley going home.
My father fits goggles to his head.

From his pocket he takes anything metal,
the pearl-handled jack knife, a ring of keys,
and for us, black money shoveled
from the sulphur pyramids heaped in the distance
like yellow gold. Coffee bottle tucked in his armpit
he swaggers past the chicken coop,
a pack of cards at his breast.
In a fan of light beyond him
the *Kino Maru* pulls out for Seattle,
some black star climbing
the deep globe of his eye.

As the oldest child, I seemed to serve my parents' lives in an ambassadorial capacity. But I was an ambassador without a country, for the household was perpetually on the verge of dissolving. I cannot say how many times I watched my father go down the walk to the picket fence, leaving us forever, pausing long enough at the gate to look back at us huddled on the porch. 'Who's coming with me?' he would ask. No one moved. Again and again we abandoned each other.

Maybe this was the making of my refugee mentality. And perhaps when you are an emotional refugee you learn to be industrious toward the prospect of love and shelter. You know both are fragile and that stability must lie with you or it is nowhere. You make a home of yourself. For me, words and later poems were the tools of that home-making.

Even when you think you are only a child and have nothing, there are things you have, and as Sartre has already told us, one of these things is words. When I saw I had words and that these could affect what happened to me and those I loved, I felt less powerless, as though words might win through, might at least mediate in a life ruled as much by chance as by intention.

These ambassadorial skills I was learning as a child were an odd kind of training for the writing of poems, perhaps, but they were just that. For in the writing of the poem you must represent both sides of the question. If not in fact, then in understanding. You must bring them into dialogue with one another fairly, without the bias of causes or indignation or needing too much to be right. It requires a widening of perspective, away from oversimplification – the strict good or bad, wrong or rightness of a situation. The sensibility I've been attempting to write out of wants to represent the spectrum of awareness. In this way the life is accounted for in its fullness, when I am able.

I have spoken of words as a stay against unreasonableness, and they are often this – though more to one's solitude than to the actual life. My father came to his own words late, but in time. I was to discover that at seventy he could entertain my poet friends and would be spoken of afterward as someone exceptional in their experience. He told stories, was witty, liked to laugh. But in those early days, my father was not a man you could talk with. He would drive me to my piano lessons, the family's one luxury, without speaking. He smoked cigarettes, one after the other. He was thinking and driving. If he had had anything to drink during these times it was best to give him a wide berth. I was often afraid of him, of the violence in him, though like the rain, tenderness was there, unspoken and with a fiber that strangely informed even the unreasonable. If to be a poet is to balance contraries, to see how seemingly opposite qualities partake of, in fact penetrate, each other, I learned this from my combative parents.

3 A.M. Kitchen: My Father Talking

For years it was land working me, oil fields,
cotton fields, then I got some land. I
worked it. Them days you could just about
make a living. I was logging.

Then I sent to Missouri. Momma
come out. We got married.
We got some kids. Five kids.
That kept us going.

We bought some land near the water.
It was cheap then. The water
was right there. You just looked out
the window. It never left the window.

I bought a boat. Fourteen-footer.
There was fish out there then.
You remember, we used to catch
six, eight fish, clean them right
out in the yard. I could of fished to China.

I quit the woods. One day just
walked out, took off my corks, said that's
it. I went to the docks.
I was driving winch. You had to watch
to see nothing fell out of the sling. If
you killed somebody you'd
never forget it. All
those years I was just working
I was on edge, every day. Just working.

You kids. I could tell you
a lot. But I won't.

It's winter. I play a lot of cards
down at the tavern. Your mother.
I have to think of excuses
to get out of the house. You're
wasting your time, she says. You're wasting
your money.

You don't have no idea, Threasie.
I run out of things
to work for. Hell, why shouldn't I
play cards? Threasie,
some days now I just don't know.

This long childhood period of living without surety contributed in another way to my urge to write poetry. If I had to give one word which serves my poetry more than any other, it might be 'uncertainty'. Uncertainty which leads to exploration, to the articulation of fears, to the loss of the kind of confidence that provides answers too quickly, too superficially. It is the poet's uncertainty which leaves her continually in an openness to the possibilities of being and saying. The true materials of poetry are essentially invisible – a capacity for the constant emptying of the house of the word, turning it out homeless and humbled to search its way toward meaning again. Maybe 'poem' for me is the act of a prolonged beginning, one without resolution except perhaps musically, rhythmically – the word 'again' engraved on the fiery hammer.

After my youngest brother's death when I was twenty, I began to recognize the ability of poetry to extend the lives of those not present except as memory. My brother's death was the official beginning of my mortality. It filled my life, all our lives, with the sense of an unspoken bond, a pain which travelled with us in memory. It was as though memory were a kind of flickering shadow left behind by those who died. This caused me to connect memory firmly to the life of the spirit and finally to write poems which formalized the sharing of that memory.

I have been writing about my progress toward a life in words and poems, but my first love was actually paint. As a child I took great pleasure in the smell of linseed, the oil of it on my fingers, the tubes of oil paint with their bands of approximate color near the caps, the long-handled brushes. I had heard somewhere that artists taught themselves by copying other painters. But the only paintings we had in the house were those in some Bible books a salesman had sold my mother. I began to copy these with oil colors onto some rough paper I'd found in a boxcar near the paper mill below our house. I remember especially my painting of Jacob sleeping at the foot of a heavenly stairway, with several angels descending. They each had a pair of huge wings, and I wondered at the time why they didn't just fly down, instead of using the stairs. The faces of these angels occupied a great deal of my efforts. And I think it is some help to being a poet to paint the faces of angels when you are ten.

I finished the Jacob painting and sent it to my grandfather in Missouri. He was a farmer and owned a thousand-acre farm of scrub oak, farmland, and river-bed in the Ozarks. My mother had been raised there. Often when she had a faraway look about her, I imagined she was visiting there in her thoughts.

My Mother Remembers That She Was Beautiful

The falling snow has made her thoughtful
and young in the privacy
of our table with its netted candle
and thick white plates. The serious faces
of the lights breathe on the pine boards
behind her. She is visiting
the daughter never close
or far enough away to come to.

She keeps her coat on, called into
her girlhood by such forgetting
I am gone or yet
to happen. She sees herself
among the townspeople, the country glances
slow with fields and sky
as she passes or waits
with a brother in the hot animal smell
of the auction stand: sunlight,
straw hats, a dog's tail
brushing her bare leg.

'There are things you know.
I didn't have to beg,' she said, 'for anything.'

The beautiful one speaks to me
from the changed, proud face and I see
how little I've let her know
of what she becomes. Years
were never the trouble, or the white hair
I braided near the sea
on a summer day. Who
she must have been
is lost to me through some fault
in my own reflection and we will have to go on
as we think we are, walking for no one's sake
from the empty restaurant into the one color
of the snow – before us, the close houses,
the brave and wondering lights of the houses.

Children sometimes adopt a second father or mother when they are cut off from the natural parent. Porter Morris, my uncle, was the father I could speak with. He lived with my grandparents on the farm in Windyville, Missouri, where I spent many of my childhood summers. He never married, but stayed with the farm even after my grandparents died. He'd been a mule trainer during the Second World War, the only time he had ever left home. He loved horses and raised and gentled one for me, which he named Angel Foot because she was black except for one white foot.

I continued to visit my grandfather and my uncle during the five years of my first marriage. My husband was a jet pilot in the Marine Corps. We were stationed in the South, so I would go to cook for my uncle during the haying and I would also help stack the hay in the barn. My uncle and I took salt to the cattle. We sowed a field with barley and went to market in Springfield with a truckload of pigs. There were visits with neighbors, Cleydeth and Joe Stefter or Jule Elliot, when we sat for hours telling stories and gossiping. Many images from my uncle's stories and from these visits to the farm got into the long poem 'Songs of the Runaway Bride' in my first book.

My uncle lived alone at the farm after my grandfather's death, but soon he met a woman who lived with her elderly parents. He began to remodel an old house on the farm. There was talk of marriage. One day my mother called to say there had been a fire at the farm. The house had burned to the ground and my uncle could not be found. She returned to the farm, what remained of her childhood home. After the ashes had cooled, she searched with the sheriff and found my uncle's skeleton where it had burned into the mattress springs of the bed.

My mother would not accept the coroner's verdict that the fire had been caused by an electrical short-circuit, or a fire in the chimney. It was summer and no fire would have been laid. She combed the ashes looking for the shot-gun my uncle always kept near his bed and the other gun, a rifle, he hunted with. They were not to be found. My mother believed her brother had been murdered and she set about proving it. She offered a reward and soon after, a young boy walking along the roadside picked my uncle's billfold out of the ditch, his name stamped in gold on the flap.

Three men were eventually brought to trial. I journeyed to Bolivar, Missouri, to meet my parents for the trial. We watched as the accused killer was released and the other two men, who had confessed to being his accomplices, were sentenced to five years in the penitentiary for manslaughter. Two years later they would be paroled. The motive had been money, although one of the men had held a grudge against my uncle for having been ordered to move out of a house he'd been renting from my uncle some three years before. They had taken forty dollars from my uncle, then shot him when he could not give them more. My parents and I came away from the trial stunned with disbelief and anger.

Two Stories

*to the author of a story taken from the death of
my uncle, Porter Morris, killed June 7, 1972*

You kept the names, the flies
of who they were, mine
gone carnival, ugly Tessie.
It got wilder but nothing
personal. The plot had me
an easy lay for a buck.
My uncle came to life
as my lover. At 16
the murderer stabbed cows
and mutilated chickens. Grown,
you gave him a crowbar that happened
to be handy twice. Then you made him
do it alone. For me

22

it took three drunks, a gun, the house
on fire. There was a black space
between trees where I told you.

The shape of my uncle
spread its arms on the wire springs
in the yard and the neighbors
came to look at his shadow
caught there under the nose
of his dog. They left that angel
to you. Your killer never
mentioned money. Like us he wanted
to outlive his hand in the sure blood
of another. The veins of my uncle streaked
where the house had been. They watched
until morning. Your man found a faucet
in an old man's side. His pants
were stiff with it for days. He left
the crowbar on Tessie's porch like a bone.

My weapon was never found.
The murderers drove a white
stationwagon and puked
as they went. They hoped
for 100 dollar bills stuffed
in a lard can. But a farmer
keeps his money in cattle
and land. They threw his billfold
into the ditch like an empty
bird. One ran away. Two stayed
with women. I kept the news
blind. You took it from my mouth,
shaped it for the market, still
a dream worse than I remembered.

Now there is the story of me
reading your story and the one
of you saying it
doesn't deserve such care.
I say it matters
that the dog stays by the chimney
for months, and a rain
soft as the sleep of cats
enters the land, emptied
of its cows, its wire gates pulled down
by hands that never dug
the single well, this whitened field.

I tried to write it out, to investigate the nature of vengeance, to disarm my-
self of the anger I carried. I wrote two poems about this event: 'Two Stories'
and 'The Absence'. Images from my uncle's death also appeared in 'Stepping
Outside', the title-poem of my first, limited-edition collection. I began to see
poems as a way of settling scores with the self. I felt I had reached the only
possible justice for my uncle in the writing out of my anger and the honoring
of the life that had been taken so brutally. The *In Cold Blood* aspect of my
uncle's murder has caused violence to haunt my vision of what it is to live in

America. Sometimes, with my eyes wide open, I still see the wall behind my grandfather's empty bed, and on it, the fiery angels and Jacob burning.

I felt if my uncle, the proverbial honest man, could be murdered in the middle of the night, then anything was possible. The intermittent hardships of my childhood were nothing compared to this. I saw how easily I could go into a state of fear and anger which would mar the energy of my life and consequently my poems for good. I think I began, in a steady way, to move toward accepting my own death, so that whenever it would come before me as a thought, I would release myself toward it. In the poems I've written that please me most, I seem able to see the experience with dead-living eyes, with a dead-living heart.

My own sense of time in poems approximates what I experience in my life – that important time junctures of past with present events via memory, with actual presences, are always inviting new meanings, revisions of old meanings, and speculation about things still in the future. These time shifts are a special province of poems because they can happen there more quickly, economically, and convincingly than in any other art form, including film. Film is still struggling to develop a language of interiority using the corporeal image, while even words like *drum* and *grief* in poems can borrow inflection from the overlap of neighboring words in context, can form entire new entities, as in a line from Louise Bogan's poem 'Summer Wish': 'the drum pitched deep as grief'.

Since my intention here has been to emphasize experiential influences rather than literary ones, I must speak of the Vietnam War, for it was the war that finally caused me to take up my life as a poet. For the first time since I had left home for college, I was thrown back on my own resources. My husband and I had met when I was eighteen and married when I was twenty-one. I was twenty-six when he left to fly missions in Vietnam. I'd had very little life on my own. It became a time to test my strengths. I began working as a ward clerk in a hospital, on the medical floor. I did this for about five months, while the news of the war arrived daily in my mailbox. I was approaching what a friend of that time called an 'eclipse'. He urged me to leave the country. It was the best decision I could have made, as I look back now.

My time in Ireland and Europe during the Vietnam War put me firmly in possession of my own life. But in doing this, it made my life in that former time seem fraudulent. The returning veterans, my husband among them, had the hardship of realizing that many Americans felt the war to be wrong. This pervasive judgment was a burden to us both and one that eventually contributed to the dissolution of our marriage.

I began to experience a kind of psychic suffocation which expressed itself in poems that I copied fully composed from my dreams. For a while, this disassociation of dream material from my life caused the messages to go unheeded. But gradually my movement out of the marriage began to enact the images of dissolution in the poems. It was a parting that gave me unresolvable grief, yet at the same time allowed my life its first true joys as I began a full commitment to my writing. I think partings have often informed my poems with a backward longing, and it was especially so with this parting from a man who has been held close at heart ever since.

24

I returned to Seattle in 1969 and began to study poetry with David Wagoner and Mark Strand at the University of Washington. My family did not understand what I was doing. Why should I divorce and then go back to college to learn to write poetry? It was beyond them. What was going to become of me now? Who would take care of me?

Trees have always been an important support to the solitude I connect with the writing of poetry. I suspect my affection and need of them began in those days of childhood when I was logging with my parents. There was a coolness in the forest, a feeling of light filtering down from the arrow-shaped tops of the evergreens. The smell of pitch comes back. The chain-saw snarl and a spray of wood chips. Sawdust in the cuffs of my jeans. My brothers and I are again the woodcutter's children. We play under the trees, but even our play is a likeness to work. We construct shelters of rotten logs, thatch them with fireweed, and then invite our parents into the shelters to eat their lunches. We eat Spam sandwiches and smoked fish, with a Mountain Bar for dessert. After a time, my parents give me a little hatchet and a marking stick so I can work with them, notching the logs to be cut up into pulpwood to be made into paper. My brothers and I strip cones from the fallen trees, milking the hard pellets with our bare hands into gunnysacks, which are sold to the Forestry Department for ten dollars a bag. There is a living to be made and all of us are expected to do our share.

When I think of it now, it is not far from the building of those makeshift shelters to the making of poems. You take what you find, what comes naturally to the hand and mind. There was the sense with these shelters that they wouldn't last, but that they were exactly what could be done at the time. There were great gaps between the logs because we couldn't notch them into each other, but this allowed us to see the greater forest between them. It was a house that remembered its forest. And for me, the best poems, no matter how much order they make, have an undercurrent of forest, of the larger unknown.

To spend one's earliest days in a forest with a minimum of supervision gave a lot of time for exploring. I also had some practice in being lost. Both exploring and being lost are, it seems now, the best kind of training for a poet. When I think of those times I was lost, they come back with a strange exhilaration, as though I had died, yet had the possibility of coming back to life. The act of writing a poem is like that. It is that sense of aloneness which is trying to locate the world again, but not too soon, not until the voice has made its cry, 'Here, here, over here,' and the answering voices have called back, 'Where are you?'

My mother and father started logging together in 1941, the year my mother travelled from Denver, Colorado, by bus to marry my father. As far as she knows, she was the only woman who worked in the woods, doing the same work men did. She was mainly the choker-setter and haul-back. She hauled the heavy steel cable, used to yard the logs into the landing, out over the underbrush to be hooked around the fallen trees. My mother's job was a dangerous one because the trees, like any dying thing, would often thrash up unexpectedly or release underbrush which could take out an eye or lodge in one's side. She also lifted and stacked the pulpwood onto the truck and helped in the trimming of the branches. She did this work for seven years.

There is a photograph of my mother sitting atop two gigantic logs in her puffed-sleeve blouse and black work pants. It has always inspired me with a pride in my sex. I think I grew up with the idea that whatever the rest of the world said about women, the woman my mother was stood equal to any man and maybe one better. Her labor was not an effort to prove anything to anyone. It was what had to be done for the living. I did not think of her as unusual until I was about fourteen. I realized then that she was a wonderful mechanic. She could fix machines, could take them apart and reassemble them. None of the mothers of my friends had such faith in their own abilities. She was curious and she taught herself. She liked to tinker, to shift a situation or an object around. She had an eye for possibilities and a faculty for intuitive decision-making that was itself a kind of knowledge. I feel I've transferred to the writing of poems many of my mother's explorative methods, even a similar audacity toward my materials.

'What happened to those letters?' I ask my mother over the telephone. I don't tell her I'm at the Dewitt Ranch Motel writing this essay. I don't tell her I'm trying to understand why I keep remembering my father's love letters as having an importance to my own writing.

'Well, a lot of them were sent to the draft board,' she says. 'Your dad and I were married November of forty-one. Pearl Harbor hit December seventh, so they were going to draft your father. A lot of men was just jumping up to get married to avoid the draft. We had to prove we'd been courting. The only way was to send the letters, so they could see for themselves.'

'But what happened to the letters?'

'There was only about three of them left. You kids got into them, so I burnt them.'

'You burnt them? Why? Why'd you do that?'

'They wasn't nothing in them.'

'But you kept them,' I say. 'You saved them.'

'I don't know why I did,' she says. 'They didn't amount to anything.'

I hang up. I sit on one of the two beds and stare out at an identical arm of the motel which parallels my unit. I think of my father's love letters being perused by the members of the draft board. They become convinced the courtship is authentic. They decide not to draft my father into the war. As a result of his having written love letters, he does not go to his death, and my birth takes place. It is an intricate chain of events, about which I had no idea at the start of this essay.

I think of my father's love letters burning, of how they might never have come into their true importance had I not returned to them here in my own writing. I sit in the motel room, a place of much passage and no record, and feel I have made an important assault on the Great Nothing, though the letters are gone, though they did not, in a sense, truly exist until this writing, even for my parents, who wrote and received them.

My father's love letters are the sign of a long courtship and I pay homage to that, the idea of writing as proof of the courtship – the same blind, persistent hopefulness that carries me again and again into poems.

Kidnaper

He motions me over with a question.
He is lost. I believe him. It seems
he calls my name. I move
closer. He says it again, the name
of someone he loves. I step back pretending

not to hear. I suspect
the street he wants
does not exist, but I am glad to point
away from myself. While he turns
I slip off my wristwatch, already laying a trail
for those who must find me
tumbled like an abandoned car
into the ravine. I lie

without breath for days among ferns.
Pine needles drift
onto my face and breasts
like the tiny hands
of watches. Cars pass.
I imagine it's him
coming back. My death
is not needed. The sun climbs again
for everyone. He lifts me
like a bride

and the leaves fall from my shoulders
in twenty-dollar bills.
'You must have been cold,' he says
covering me with his handkerchief.
'You must have given me up.'

Instructions to the Double

So now it's your turn,
little mother of silences, little
father of half-belief. Take up
this face, these daily rounds
with a cabbage under each arm

convincing the multitudes
that a well-made-anything
could save them. Take up
most of all, these hands
trained to an ornate piano
in a house on the other side
of the country.

I'm staying here
without music, without
applause. I'm not going
to wait up for you. Take
your time. Take mine
too. Get into some trouble
I'll have to account for. Walk
into some bars alone
with a slit in your skirt. Let
the men follow you on the street
with their clumsy propositions, their
loud hatreds of this and that. Keep
walking. Keep your head
up. They are calling to you – slut, mother,
virgin, whore, daughter, adultress, lover,
mistress, bitch, wife, cunt, harlot,
betrothed, Jezebel, Messalina, Diana,
Bathsheba, Rebecca, Lucretia, Mary,
Magdelena, Ruth, you – Niobe,
woman of the tombs.

Don't stop for anything, not
a caress or a promise. Go
to the temple of the poets, not
the one like a run-down country club,
but the one on fire
with so much it wants
to be done with. Say all the last words
and the first: hello, goodbye, yes,
I, no, please, always, never.

If anyone from the country club
asks if you write poems, say
your name is Lizzie Borden.
Show him your axe, the one
they gave you with a silver
blade, your name engraved there
like a whisper of their own.

If anyone calls you a witch,
burn for him; if anyone calls you
less or more than you are
let him burn for you.

It's a dangerous mission. You
could die out there. You
could live forever.

Breasts

The day you came
this world got its hold on me.
Summer grass and the four of us pounding hell
out of each other for god knows what
green murder of the skull.
Swart nubbins, I noticed you then,
my mother shaking a gritty rag from the porch
to get my shirt on this minute. Brothers,
that was the parting of our ways, for then
you got me down by something else than flesh.
By the loose skin of a cotton shirt
you kept me to the ground
until the bloody gout hung in my face like a web.

Little mothers, I can't find your children.
I have looked in a man
who moved through the air like a god.
He brought me clouds
and the loose stars of his goings.
Another kissed me on a pier in Georgia
but there was blood on his hands,
bad whiskey in the wind. The last one,
he made me a liar until I stole
what I could not win. Loves,
what is this mirror you have left me in?

I could have told you at the start
there would be trouble
from other hands, how the sharp mouths
would find you where you slept.

But I have hurt you as certainly
with cold sorrowings as anyone,
have come the long way
over broken ground to this softness.
Good clowns, how could I know, all along
it was your blundering mercies kept me alive
when heaven was a luckless dream.

The Woman Who Raised Goats

Dear ones, in those days it was otherwise.
I was suited more to an obedience
of windows. If anyone had asked,
I would have said: 'Windows are my prologue.'

My father worked on the docks
in a cold little harbor, unhappily
dedicated to what was needed
by the next and further
harbors. My brothers
succeeded him in this, but when I,
in that town's forsaken luster, offered myself,
the old men in the hiring hall creeled
back in their chairs, fanning themselves
with their cards, with their gloves.
'Saucy,' they said. 'She's saucy!'

Denial, O my Senators,
takes a random shape. The matter
drove me to wearing
a fedora. Soon, the gowns, the amiable
forgeries: a powdery sailor, the blue silk
pillow given by a great aunt, my name
embroidered on it like a ship, the stitched
horse too, with its red plume and its bird eyes
glowing, glowing. There was the education
of my 'sensibilities'.

All this is nothing to you.
You have eaten my only dress, and the town
drifts every day now
toward the harbor. But always,

34

above the town, above
the harbor, there is the town,
the harbor, the caves and hollows
when the cargo of lights
is gone.

Beginning to Say No

is not to offer so much as a fist, is
to walk away firmly, as though
you had settled something foolish,
is to wear a tarantula in your buttonhole
yet smile invitingly, unmindful
how your own blood grows toward the irreversible
bite. No, I will not

go with you. No, that is not
all right. I'm not your sweet-dish, your
home-cooking, good-looking daf-
fodil. Yes is no
reason to slay the cyclops. No
will not save it. And the cricket, 'Yes, yes.'

Fresh bait, fresh bait!
The search for the right hesitation
includes finally
unobstructed waters. Goodbye,
old happy-go-anyhow, old shoe
for any weather. Whose
candelabra are you? Whose
soft-guy, nevermind, nothing-to-lose ant hill?

'And,' the despised connective,
is really an engine
until it is *yes* all day, until a light
is thrown against a wall
with some result. And
there is less doubt, yes or no,
for whatever you have been compelled to say
more than once.

Coming Home

As usual, I was desperate.
I went through your house as if I owned it.
I said, 'I need This, This and This.'
But contrary to all I know of you,
you did not answer, only looked after me.

I've never seen the house so empty, Mother.
Even the rugs felt it, how little
they covered. And what have you done
with the plants? How thankfully
we thought their green replaced us.

You were keeping something like a light.
I had seen it before, a place you'd never been
or never come back from. It was a special way
your eyes looked out over the water. Whitecaps
lifted the bay and you said, 'He should be here
by now.'

How he always came back; the drinking,
the fishing into the night, all
the ruthless ships he unloaded.
That was the miracle of our lives. Even now
he won't stay out of what I have
to say to you.

But they worry me, those boxes
of clothes I left in your basement. Sometimes
I think of home as a storehouse, the more
we leave behind, the less
you say. The last time
I couldn't take anything.

So I'm always coming back like tonight,
in a temper, brushing the azaleas
on the doorstep. What did you mean
by it, this tenderness
that is a whip, a longing?

Black Money

His lungs heaving all day in a sulphur mist,
then dusk, the lunch pail torn from him
before he reaches the house, his children
a cloud of swallows about him.
At the stove in the tumbled rooms, the wife,
her back the wall he fights most, and she
with no weapon but silence
and to keep him from the bed.

In their sleep the mill hums and turns
at the edge of water. Blue smoke
swells the night and they drift
from the graves they have made for each other,
float out from the open-mouthed sleep
of their children, past banks and businesses,
the used car lots, liquor store, the swings in the park.

The mill burns on, now a burst of cinders,
now whistles screaming down the bay, saws jagged
in half light. Then like a whip
the sun across the bed, windows high with mountains
and the sleepers fallen to pillows
as gulls fall, tilting
against their shadows on the log booms.
Again the trucks shudder the wood-framed houses
passing to the mill. My father
snorts, splashes in the bathroom,
throws open our doors to cowboy music
on the radio. Hearts are cheating,
somebody is alone, there's blood in Tulsa.
Out the back yard the night-shift men rattle
the gravel in the alley going home.
My father fits goggles to his head.

From his pocket he takes anything metal,
the pearl-handled jack knife, a ring of keys,
and for us, black money shoveled
from the sulphur pyramids heaped in the distance
like yellow gold. Coffee bottle tucked in his armpit
he swaggers past the chicken coop,
a pack of cards at his breast.

In a fan of light beyond him
the *Kino Maru* pulls out for Seattle,
some black star climbing
the deep globe of his eye.

Clearing

The limbs are caught in each other
outside my window where the men
have entered the tree. Dead limbs
pile up on the shadows.
Now a saw goes up on a rope
and the ground man steps back
for what falls. I tell him my father
rigged spar trees in the west.
I need a reason to watch
this tree come down.

He uses his weight on the rope
like a saw, then backs off.
The chainsaw snarls and jaws.
Over him, the tree and the wind: sawdust
over my house.

If a tree goes down among others
it makes its whole length felt
as something lost and final, not
this slow dispossession
of parts. I have heard a whole tree cry out
in the clearings my father made.
But this tree snaps and shudders
and calms itself back
into silence.

From the street, the houses
seem to have stepped away.

In my window the likeness
of the tree goes on, the light
opening and gathering
over my desk, over what I cannot heal.

Even Now You Are Leaving

Not to let ourselves know
by a hand held too long, as this last,
words no part of any other, like a mule
trained to carry anything
and not mean it. Just so these lips
puffed from where you ran into yourself
in a car the night before, the wheel
turning through your mouth
like something you might have said.

I can't believe your face, that
it could fall from here, let alone
my own. Yet you prove it, the chin
large now as a forehead. Some nearness
has done this to you, or the lack
of it. That scheme you had
for making us rich, I want to tell you
it worked, though Alaska
stayed due north
and you never touched.

The spar tree axe
swings from a tree you rigged
to hold that clearing. I can't look up.
The tree's too white
and cedar an easy fire. Father,
some neglect is killing us all, but yours
has a name of its own: family,
something gone on without you, your eyes
ruined and terrible in a face
even now you are leaving.

The Coats

(for my grandmother, Mary Kepler Bond, 1884-1966*)*

They made you complicated,
a new one each year
and underneath, the same
old print dress. Outside
under the maples you were smart
and garrulous on my grandfather's arm
walking down Valley Street
to the shops, talking into his silence
as into some idea of yourself
grown to your side.

Yet you loved telling how
you were engaged to another
the night he took you off
in his buckboard. Marriage too
came like an impulse
to turn against yourself. Life
caught you up in its clumsy arms
and danced you out of your Oklahoma
youth into the milltown
of my birth, you in your new coat,
leading me into the dimestore
to buy silk ribbons.

Shut in the closet, your coats
were a family of witnesses
who could not remember you.
They were waiting for the one
to send them all again
into the weather. Standing
before your mirror once
in the dark of the bedroom
I put myself into a heavy tweed
with its cold silk lining. The wide arms
were a hiding place; the hem
brushed my patent leather shoes.
It was a bargaining
that I should turn into the room,
your age about me like a sack.

I wanted to throw something over you
the day they carried you off
like a trophy in your silk lining.
Rosy and familiar you received each of us
in a housedress that denied you
were going anywhere. That year
the winter came over the ground
like a rich white pelt.
I thought of you accepting it,
something chosen, a comfort
that had sought you out
in the cold of the land.

The Horse in the Drugstore

wants to be admired.
He no longer thinks of what he has given up
to stand here, the milk-white reason
of chickens over his head in the night, the grass
spilling on through the day. No, it is enough
to stand so with his polished chest among the nipples
and bibs, the cotton, and multiple sprays, with his black lips
parted just slightly and the forehooves doubled back
in the lavender air. He has learned when maligned to snort
dimes and to carry the inscrutable bruise like a bride.

Cows, a Vision

(for Porter Morris)

Some monster bird, the barn
flings its shadow across the field
to the walnut grove. The cows
with milk-worn bodies muffle
its cry, the cry of riverbeds
gone white. In the rafters
the wings of swallows breathe
over eggs like eyes. If the sun
falls on them they must open
and fly. I was born that way,
some beak of light lifting a straw.

The cows were never·born. They came
with the land, with the bucket
hanging in the well, with the iron
bed and the empty cat who slept
by the clock and ticked only
to your hand. You took it all
because it was the cat's dream
or the clock's or the empty bed
waiting. You filled everything,
the barn, the bucket, the bed,
even the empty dream and then
you built yourself a front porch
where, of an evening, you could
sit down to bullfrogs and rusty owls.

It was up to the cows after that
to keep things going. Their mouths
were always faithful, turning
like windmills the heavy heart
of the moon. For a moment toward dawn
or dusk the cows pause in their work
and a secret moon swells in them,
threatens to carry them over the barn
and away. When we die, I tell you,
that moon will find its stars and nothing
will keep them down. You aren't worried.
For you there is only more good land.

When You Speak to Me

Take care when you speak to me.
I might listen, I might
draw near as the flame
breathing with the log, breathing
with the tree it has not
forgotten. I might
put my face
next to
your face
in your nameless trouble,
in your trouble
and name.

It is a thing I learned
without learning; a hand
is a stronger mouth, a kiss could
crack the skull, these
words, small steps
in the air calling
the secret hands, the mouths
hidden in the flesh.

This isn't robbery.
This isn't your blood for my
tears, no confidence
in trade or barter. I may
say nothing back
which is to hear
after you the fever
inside the words we say
apart, the words we say so hard
they fall apart.

A Poem in Translation

After years smuggling poems
out of an unknown country,
you have been discovered by a known

and skillful master. Your language
is foreign and eligible, your circumstances
Russian, complete with prison camps
and midnight journeys by train
through the Urals. Someone is always taking
your hand as a stranger, entrusting you
with a few saved belongings
before he is led away.

You too are led, a pair of eyes
wearing sight like an armor.
You witness it all. You do not suffer
the physical shame, your clothes
taken from you, your body
made to stand with the weeping others.
Somehow you are not harmed.
You stitch a cry into the hem of your coat
to be unravelled in a land of comfort.

They work over the lines like a corpse
taken from the ground. Gradually
they heap their own flesh
over what has remained,
the beautiful gaps and silences.

In the new language you are awkward.
You don't agree with yourself,
these versions of what you *meant*
to say. Like a journalist, one has written
'throat' where you have said
'throat'. Another uses his ears
as a mouth; he writes like an orator
in a bathroom, not 'tears'
but 'sobbing'.

Still another has only heard your name
and the title of one poem
full of proper names, rivers
and cities no one bothers
to translate. All his poems begin here
and move into the dream of you
as the ideal sacrifice, redeeming him
from a language he knows too well
to say anything simply.

One night (it always happens at night)
these translations, against all precautions,
are smuggled back to you by a woman
looking much like yourself. She
takes your hand and leads you away
into a room where each one calls you
by his name and you enter the solitary
kingdom of your face.

Stepping Outside
(for Akhmatova)

Hearing of you, I never lost a brother
though I have, never saw a husband to war,
though I have, never kept with my father
the emptiness of his hands, my mother
the dying of her womb.

Return: husbands, sons, fathers return.
Many with both arms, with dreams
broken in both eyes.
They try, they try
but they cannot tell us
what comes back with them.

One more has planted his hoe
in my heart like an axe, my farmer uncle
slain by thieves
in the night, burned down
with his house, buried, dug up
to prove he was no dog.
He was no dog.

You, who lived in your pain until it grew
its own face, would have left all this
like a monument in a field. Your words
would have made a feast of what ate you.

Sit with me.
No one has left; no one returns.

Time Lapse with Tulips

(for Michael Burkard)

That kiss meant to sear my heart forever –
it went right by.
And the way we walked out on Sundays
to the bakery, like a very old couple, arm
on arm, that's gone too
though the street had a house with a harp
in the window.

Those tulips again.
They think if they keep being given away
by the black-haired man at our wedding
I will finally take them in time
for the photograph. But they are wrong.
This time I will hand them back or leave them
sitting in the Mason jar
on the grass beside you.

See how the guests lean after me, their mouths
slightly open. Only now it's plain
they were never sure, that the picture
holding us all preserves
a symmetry of doubt with us
at the center, the pledge
of tulips red against my dress.

Whatever the picture says, it is wrong.
I take my image back, the white
petals that were standing a while at your side,
petals falling a while
at your side. Here instead,
the trick of flesh held again to your cheek.
Inside, the rare bone of my hand and that harp
seen through a window suddenly so tempting

you must rush into that closed room, you must
tear your fingers across it.

Croce e Delizia al Cor

Remember, and already the lapse in
vision pulls you back
too suddenly, the swing lowering
the boughs of the ash. You could sail forever
through the side of some fundamental right
you were giving yourself
at his expense.

The swing repeats the arc, the air
under you. Crouched
in a moving corner, this looking down
makes you feel specially weighted for falling,
an urge to get between assassinations
of either fixity, sky or ground.

Where you tempt the arc to be happy on its own,
the baby's buggy careens down cloudless skies
breaking your eyeglasses, both lenses at
once. So the frame presents the eyes
in a harmony not understood as the harbor
falls away through ships.

This necessity of returns
prolongs everything. The tree belongs to the
lawn, though the swing, it's true, is artificial,
heading like that over the girl in braids
eating a peanut butter sandwich near
the fence. She is inventing her turn
while the parents rub up against
our house in a paroxysm of bad advice. They
would praise the swing if it subdued
the tree. And yes, because you didn't look away,
something was settled.

Just then your mother steps out
of the lilac, meaning to leave you
with a last word. Call it a continuous hesitation,
her not wanting to admit pain which demands
credit and balance. 'Anyone, after all, can let things
go to hell,' before the sun
smashes the horizon and you catch sight of the
buggy hurtling impossibly through an entire
generation of good intentions.

The harbor yawns in and
out. Behind, into branches, the nest
is a sky broken from you. It matches that holding
the ships just above water.
Even so, the baby will drown there on the lawn
with the broken lenses, the blur of intimate
conjunctions: that bird dying into the sweep of
your knees above the houses.

The Calm

(for Lawrence Gallagher)

We were walking through the bees
and stars. Our mouths
made a sense without us.
I loved your hands
because of your mouth, each star
because of a life not chosen
by the hand. I told you,
don't say it, the loss
of our lives beyond us. You
said it. You said it
for the sake of a loneliness
together, for the praise of our eyes
going on without shadows.

Even now, when all our nights
have washed away
and the apples have left
the trees, I am keeping your place
where the high grass
has entered the song. Like a swarm,
the heart moves with its separate
wings under the eaves.

If I knew where to find you
I would say goodbye
and have the hurtful ease of that,
but the gates are everywhere
and this calm – an imagined forgiveness,
the childhood before we meet again.

Corona

Personable shadow, you follow me into this
daylight-dream, the one even my body
knows nothing of.

This flesh is your halo, the meat you drag daily
across the earth like an injured
wife. The sun

surrounds us as the heart surrounds
the body. Let us
navigate each pleasure, each pain

like a doorway, its ambush: the mouth, the bouquet,
the six-story ladder, that
memory of a train

missed in Budapest, everything passing through.
The tail of a shirt
caresses the back of my brother who falls again

from the tractor in 1957. A woman's body
flies out of the house
like an insult. It is the day we are found

missing. See
the windows floating beside us into the next world,
admitting they don't know what they're for.

I will speak to you like a lover, not as one
I have used
to keep from being true. This water is a memory

of sleep folding us
under. Your face
covers mine; the moon of your face blasted from a train

through faults of light in the trees – again and
again cut off, this water
taking up our hands.

Zero

Stupid tranquility, to be most sure
in the abstract, the zebra
raising its head from the river, the clock
wound to the usual multitude, the junco bird
appearing as a miracle on the blind magician's
balcony. A thing among things,
the magician is there as an absolute, his
long sleeves, an attitude of sight
that amounts to seeing, the morning steady

in the orange grove. To sit with him
is to sense the luminous sides
of objects making a finite path
to an infinite doorway. See how he multiplies
himself like the doves in his hat,
not flying away into the village
but resting in the white brocade
on the crook of his arm.

He walks the promenade, a procession
of explicit consequences, the funeral
climbing the hill with its tub
of roses. Magic powder clings
to his tongue, alum and ginger. A mild
contraction in the landscape, his reticence
to prove himself. Doesn't the sun
look as if it got there again
over the handkerchief snake
in his palm? This knot could make you cry,
how it slips past itself, now a
bracelet, now a white stem
drawn in the serious air of your breath,
letting itself down, the careful
ballerina closing the halo
of her partner's arms.

Snowheart

In our houses, the snow keeps us
travelling. It says: your life
is where you are. The phone,
all day ringing by itself
over the next lot, isn't for you.

The man with the perfect
haircut makes a track
across the lawn, holding
his books like a
breast. *Snowheart*

you have said: *don't cut your black hair.*

Love's the only debt.
He's up again
and riding the best mare
ten miles by moonlight, the
spruce-backed fiddle
under his arm.

'Dance us the next one too.
If day comes, don't
tell. Let the horse
go home alone.'

Snowheart. Someone's horse
circles the near house.
There is snow
on its back.

Rhododendrons

(for my mother)

Like porches they trust their attachments,
or seem to, the road and the trees
leaving them open from both sides.
I have admired their spirit,
wild-headed women of the roadside,
how exclusion is only something glimpsed,
the locomotive dream that learns to go on
without caring for the landscape.

There is a spine in the soil
I have not praised enough:
its underhair of surface
clawed to the air. Elsewhere each shore
recommends an ease of boats, shoulders
nodding over salmon
who cross this sky with our faces.

I was justifying my confusion
the last time we walked this way.
I think I said some survivals need
a forest. But it was only the sound
of knowing. Assumptions
about roots put down like a deeper foot
seemed dangerous too.

These were flowers you did not cut,
iris and mums a kindness enough.
Some idea of relative dignities, I suppose,
let us spare each other; I came away
with your secret consent and this
lets you stand like a grief
telling itself over and over.

Even grief has instructions,
like the boats gathering light
from the water and the separate
extensions of the roots. So remembering
is only one more way of being alone
when the voice has gone everywhere
in the dusk of the porches
looking for the last thing to say.

FROM **UNDER STARS**
(1978)

What Cathál Said

'You can sing sweet
and get the song sung
but to get to the third dimension
you have to sing it
rough, hurt the tune a little. Put
enough strength to it
that the notes slip. Then
something else happens. The song
gets large.'

Words Written Near a Candle

If I could begin anything
I'd say stop asking forgiveness, especially
theirs which was always
the fault mentioned in your condition.

Nettles could be feathers
the moment they brush your
ankle. At the same time: floods, earthquakes,
the various slaveries
hunchbacked near the fence
to catch your glance.

What is it to say that among the hired boats
we carried our bodies well, cracked
jokes, left the gaps
in our lives and not
the page? This far to learn
the boat does not touch the water!

And if this is goodbye,
it is a light nowhere near believing
and I am happy
and it is all right to make a distance
of a nearness, to say, 'Boat, I have left you
behind. Boat,
I am with you.'

Women's Tug of War at Lough Arrow

In a borrowed field they dig in their feet
and clasp the rope. Balanced
against neighboring women, they hold
the ground by the little gained
and leaning like boatmen rowing into
the damp earth, they pull
to themselves the invisible waves, waters
overcalmed by desertion
or the narrow look trained to a brow.

The steady rain has made girls of them,
their hair in ringlets. Now they haul
the live weight to the cries
of husbands and children, until the rope
runs slack, runs free
and all are bound again by the arms
of those who held them, not until, but so
they gave.

Four Dancers at an Irish Wedding

It was too simple and too right,
the father blue-eyed
and doting, his daughter a mock-up
of the bride in her long dress, earrings
and matching steps.

Red shirt, I am right
for you, wrong for you. Here
is my cheek forever
in this careless waltz
where we chanced to meet.

Darling, darling, darling

in the sob-throated beat
and we are true, my sad-eyed partner,
truest to complicate the step, taking
this father's hand, this child's.

The circle opens and closes
where our joined hands meet. Sweet
gladness, I
am not yours
and you are not mine. Break. Break
where the beat widens, take
the worried girl, leave me
the father.

we are all stolen and grieving
in the tender arms.
I have seen the magpie in the morning
on the back of a cow
singing: One
is for sorrow. One
is for sorrow.

Drop the strange hand, be
lifted, child, held
there on your father's swaying shoulder
for we are one and one and
one with ourselves
on the polished floor.

The Ritual of Memories

When your widow had left the graveside
and you were most alone
I went to you in that future
you can't remember yet. I brought
a basin of clear water where no tear
had fallen, water gathered like grapes
a drop at a time
from the leaves of the willow. I brought
oils, I brought a clean white gown.

'Come out,' I said, and you came up
like a man pulling himself out of a river,
a river with so many names
there was no word left for it but 'earth'.

'Now,' I said, 'I'm ready. These eyes
that have not left your face
since the day we met, wash these eyes.
Remember, it was a country road
above the sea and I was passing
from the house of a friend. Look
into these eyes where we met.'

I saw your mind go back through the years
searching for that day and finding it,
you washed my eyes
with the pure water
so that I vanished from that road
and you passed a lifetime
and I was not there.

So you washed every part of me
where any look or touch
had passed between us. 'Remember,'
I said, when you came to the feet,
'it was the night before you would ask
the girl of your village to marry. I
was the strange one. I was the one
with the gypsy look.
Remember how you stroked these feet.'

When the lips and the hands
had been treated likewise and the pit
of the throat where one thoughtless kiss
had fallen, you rubbed in the sweet oil
and I glistened like a new-made thing, not
merely human, but of the world gone past
being human.

'The hair,' I said. 'You've forgotten
the hair. Don't you know it remembers.
Don't you know it keeps everything. Listen,
there is your voice and in it the liar's charm
that caught me.'

You listened. You heard your voice
and a look of such sadness
passed over your dead face that I wanted
to touch you. Who could have known
I would be so held? Not you
in your boyish cunning; not me
in my traveller's clothes.

It's finished.
Put the gown on my shoulders.
It's no life in the shadow of another's joys.
Let me go freely now.
One life I have lived for you. This one
is mine.

As If It Happened

She was brought up manly for a woman
to dread the tender word.
All afternoon saying goodbye
in the high-ceilinged room, he
in the rocker, its fixed
reach, the whiskey troubling
their glasses.

The dull pull of the light fanned
and narrowed between them.
She had on the red handkerchief shirt.
They talked, the memory of that, two
made fearless and humble
as those who visit the dying, their live gifts
that need tending.

Say of them: 'They were lovers once'
though little stays of that.
Yet didn't the body speak? Didn't it
fly out of its heart, its faithless
goldfish of a heart? Didn't it find your house,
opened by moonlight, walking up to it,
like a masterpiece of regret: only arms, only
the bodies of so many kisses
loosed like birds against the windows, falling.

And if that night happened, if one night
I walked up to your house shared by then
with another, wouldn't you
know me? Wouldn't you
remember one night when we were holy and helpless
in each other and wouldn't you start up then
like one in terror who has dreamed himself
backwards, dreaming he could not help stepping out
at the wrong and irrevocable moment – you
stepped out.

Now they're past recalling
and that night revolves like a planet forsaken
of its days and years. Of the two
who can tell which now
is retreating, which
has stepped this way?

On Your Own

How quickly the postures shift.
Just moments ago we seemed human,
or in the Toledo of my past
I made out I was emotionally illiterate
so as not to feel a pain I deserved.

Here at the Great Southern
some of the boys have made it
into gray suits and pocket calculators.
I'm feeling end-of-season, like a somebody
who's hung around the church
between a series of double weddings.

Friend, what you said about the terror
of American Womanhood,
I forget it already, but I know
what you mean. I'm so scary some days
I'd run from myself. It's hard work
having your way, even
half the time, and having it,
know what not to do with it. Who
hasn't thrown away a life or two
at the mercy of another's passion,
spite or industry.

It's like this on your own: the charms
unlucky, the employment
solitary, the best love always
the benefit of a strenuous doubt.

Woman-Enough

Figures on a silent screen,
they move into my window, its facing
on the abbey yard, six men with spades
and long-handled shovels. I had looked up
as I look up now across the strand where a small boat
has drifted into the haze of mountains
or that child walks to the end
of a dock.

Both views let in sun.
The bearded one throws off his coat
and rolls his sleeves. Two in their best clothes
from offices in London lean against a stone,
letting the shovels lift and slap.
The others dodge in and out of sun, elbow-high,
the ground thickening. The boat,
closer, one oar flashing,

pulled to the light and under, these voices
a darker blade. A wind
carries over and I hear him call out to me: 'He
was a wild one in his young days. You'll want
to lock your door.' He nods the bottle
to bring me out.

A drink to you, Peter Harte, man
that I never knew, lover
of cattle and one good woman
buried across the lake.
'He was a tall man, about my size,' the one
measuring, face down in the gap.
'And wouldn't you like a big man? Big
as me?' dusting his hands on his pants and lifted out.
'Try it on, go down.'

The sky, the stone blue
of the sky. An edge of faces, hard looks
as though they'd hauled me live
into the open boat of their deaths, American woman,
man-enough in that country place
to stand with skulls sifted and stacked
beside the dirt pile, but woman then
where none had stood and them more men
for that mistake to see me
where he would lay.

'Not a word of this to Mary, ye hear.'

O he was a wild one,
a wild one in his youth. Sonny Peter
Harte.

The Ballad of Ballymote

We stopped at her hut
on the road to Ballymote
but she did not look up
and her head was on her knee.

What is it, we asked.
As from the dreams of the dead
her voice came up.

My father, they shot him
as he looked up from his plate
and again as he stood and again
as he fell against the stove
and like a thrush his breath
bruised the room
and was gone.

A traveller would have asked directions
but saw she would not lift her face.
What is it, he asked.

My husband sits all day in a pub
and all night and I may as well
be a widow for the way he beats me
to prove he's alive.

What is it, asked the traveller's wife,
just come up to look.

My son's lost both eyes in a fight
to keep himself a man
and there he sits behind the door
where there is no door
and he sees by the stumps
of his hands.

And have you no daughters for comfort?

Two there are and gone to nuns
and a third to the North
with a fisherman.

What are you cooking?

Cabbage and bones, she said. Cabbage
and bones.

Disappearances in the Guarded Sector

(for Ciarán Carson)

When we stop where you lived, the house
has thickened, the entry
level to the wall with bricks, as though
it could keep you out.

Again the dream has fooled you into waking
and we have walked out
past ourselves, through the windows
to be remembered in the light
of closed rooms
as a series of impositions
across the arms of a chair, that woman's face
startled out of us so it lingers
along a brick front.

You are leading me back to the burned arcade
where you said I stood with you
in your childhood last night, your childhood
which includes me now
as surely as the look of that missing face
between the rows of houses.

We have gone so far into your past
that nothing reflects us.
No sun gleams from the glassless frame
where a room burned,
though the house stayed whole. There
is your school, your church,
the place you drank cider at lunch time.
New rows of houses are going up.
Children play quietly in a stairwell.

Walking back, you tell the story
of the sniper's bullet
making two clean holes in the taxi, how
the driver ducked and drove on
like nothing happened. No pain
passed through you; it
did not even stop the car
or make you live more
carefully. Near the check point we
stop talking, you let the hands
rub your clothes
against your body. You seem to be
there, all there.

Watching, I am more apart
for the sign of dismissal they will give me,
thinking a woman would not conceal,
as I have, the perfect map
of this return where I have met
and lost you willingly
in a dead and living place.

Now when you find me next in the dream,
this boundary will move with us.
We will both come back.

[Belfast, Winter 1976]

Open Fire Near a Shed

In the cab there was a song.
Not one I would have chosen, but
of which I remember, in my way,
some words without the tune. Also,
the driver, his coat. How is it
that the wrinkles in his coat-back
were almost tender? His small hands
taking from yours
my belongings.

You're stepping back now
behind the gray slats
of the gate. Your hand, the right
one, lifts through
the fine rain, causing me
to look back at myself
as your memory – a constancy
with its troubled interior
under the rained-on glass.

Looking out, I've moved already
into thought. The tunnel
on the train gives and returns my face
flickering across the winter fields,
the fields – their soft holdings
of water, of cows breathing warmly
over the tracks of birds.

Sudden then as light to the pane –
an open fire near a shed,
wilder in the stubble and light rain
for how it seems intended
to burn there
though no one is standing by.

Love Poem to Be Read to an Illiterate Friend

I have had to write this down
in my absence and yours. These
things happen. Thinking
of a voice added
I imagine a sympathy outside us
that protects the message
from what can't help
being said.

The times you've kept
your secret, putting on
glasses or glancing into a page
with interest, give again
the hurt you've forgiven, pretending
to be one of us.
So the hope of love
translates as a series of hidden moments
where we like to think
someone was fooled
into it.

Who was I then
who filled these days
with illegible warnings: the marriages
broken, the land
pillaged by speculators, no word
for a stranger?

This island
where I thought the language was mine
has left me lonely
and innocent as you or that friend

who let you copy his themes
until the words became pictures
of places you would never go.

Forgive it then
that so much of after
depends on these, the words
which must find you
off the page.

Second Language
(for Ciarán)

Outside, the night is glowing
with earth and rain, and you
in the next room take up
your first language.
All day it has waited
like a young girl in a field.
Now she has stood up
from the straw-flattened circle
and you have taken her glance
from the hills.

The words come back.
You are with yourself again
as that child who gave up the spoon,
the bed, the horse to its colors
and uses. There is yet no hint
they would answer to anything else
and your tongue does not multiply the wrong,
the stammer calling them back
and back.

You have started the one word
again, again as though it had to be made
a letter at a time
until it mends itself into saying.
The girl is beside you as lover or mother or
the aunt who visited with a kindly face
and the story of your mother
as a girl in a life before you.

She leads you across that field
to where the cows put down their wet lips
to the rust-dry trough.
But before you can get there
it will have changed. The water
will have two names
in and out of the ground. The song
you are singing, its familiar words and measures,
will be shadowed and bridged.

Remember the tune for the words.
Remember the cows for the field, those
in their sacred look who return
their great heads to the centuries of grass.

Out of sleep you are glad
for this rain, are steadied by my staying awake.
The trough will fill
and it will seem as though the dream
completes its far side.

To speak is to be robbed and clothed,
this language always mine
because so partly yours. Each word
has a crack in it to show the strain
of all it holds, all that leaks
away. Silent now, as when another
would think you sullen or
absent, you smoke after a meal, the sign
of food still on the plate, the two
chairs drawn away and angled again
into the room.

The rain enters, repeating its single word
until our bodies in their store-bought clothes
make a sound against us, the dangerous visit
of the flesh perfecting its fears
and celebrations, drinking us in
by the slow unspeakable syllables.

I have forced up the screen
and put out the palm of my hand past the rush
of the eaves. In the circular glow of the porch
the lighted rain is still, is falling.

Still Moment at Dún Laoghaire

(for my sister, Stevie)

You cross the ramp, its sure suspension
above the blue rope net
that means water not seen
for this nearness of ship to dock.
Now it is below you, a channel
you will think of as an ocean
where we met once and talked back
into a lost continent, childhood,
and a single house that keeps us sisters.

You were right to call it a language,
the way I will know that tree
blocking the view of the peninsula
and the bluff dropping away each year
so the house must stand with conviction
flanked by the blue spruce, the swing set
waiting for our brothers' children.

Already we are more together
for how the house looks back on us.
Through the glass your face will float away
like a ship of its own
over the boundary that knows with us
the world is steady
in another view.

Look back. There is a woman
beside me, younger, older, waving
as you are waving yet,
with your blonde hair
wound and pinned, into this distance.

Ever After

(for Yvonne McDonagh-Gaffney)

Exactly like a rain cloud
over the picnickers at the Abbey Ballindoon
or a boat reflecting

on the peak of itself without an oar, so
my death reached everything in my mind
effortlessly.

This amazed my normal appearance,
which went on swallowing
an excessive quantity of rain. An odd
expression of joy. Great sheets
of rain. Then passing

I caught the words of the mourners
like a skirt waving backwards on a scarlet road
and among them, the girl who would lay
beside me.

The long-handled shovel
from dawn to dark like a machine
and she one soft touch
for the gulls to swoop at. Cloth
buttons.

We looked at the red lights
wandering over the masts of the ships,
their dark facings in the brain,
the trees climbing side by side
with the sky into that exchange of worlds, her
hair flowing over
the river-wall. Her life, she said,

an imaginary bird let go in the white water
of January. Water that lapped
the doorstep, her short legs, her hand
on the window sill near the bridge, near
the look of the gulls
floating between the timbers.

Closing the fact of it, think
of her dead, think of a skeleton
you could embrace as the lack
of your being or lying
in this field to talk through the cry of water
into the whole future
which brings back the hands
free and ready. Think

of her. That's better. She
was at my side, the memory of her. The
wetness of the sea. I
explained to her: because you are alive
the horizon recedes. You thought you were
everything, a drum with affection, the sort
of girl to mark that page
because one hand held another
or you could skip it altogether.

If I were everything, there would be nothing
beside me. You
are beside me. The sort of girl
she was, looking out at me
through the lattices
of her hair, her
live hair.

Under Stars

The sleep of this night deepens
because I have walked coatless from the house
carrying the white envelope.
All night it will say one name
in its little tin house by the roadside.

I have raised the metal flag
so its shadow under the roadlamp
leaves an imprint on the rain-heavy bushes.
Now I will walk back
thinking of the few lights still on
in the town a mile away.

In the yellowed light of a kitchen
the millworker has finished his coffee,
his wife has laid out the white slices of bread
on the counter. Now while the bed they have left
is still warm, I will think of you, you
who are so far away
you have caused me to look up at the stars.

70

Tonight they have not moved
from childhood, those games played after dark.
Again I walk into the wet grass
toward the starry voices. Again, I
am the found one, intimate, returned
by all I touch on the way.

The Meeting
(for Ken Schar)

My name is not my own
and you are lost in the sameness
of yours: marriage, divorce,
marriage, the name changed
like a billboard at the side of my life.

That day I saw you last
you were wearing a white suit
in the mid-winter haze.
It was too big for you.
Your shoulders didn't belong.
I heard you: 'If you feel
the rightness of a thing, do it.'

Twelve years we've come
and not a word between us.
Last night you got off a bus
in my dream. Your body
seemed too small for itself. It was
hurt by something outside my sleep.
You took off your coat.
I could see the bones of your arms.
We didn't mention it.
You asked for something ordinary
and wrong, vitamins, I think.

You had your camera on your chest
like a complicated doorknob.
You didn't open.
My hands came back
to me. I was awake in that last café

where I did not say *brother*, where
I stood apart from your sorrow
in my great young indifference.

Tired lives had run you out.
You were going away. 'Let them
have their bastard courage!'
Your hands came back
to you. You touched me, that hand
out of the grave. Early
and late, this hour has closed
around us.

Harmless Streets

(for Kent Anderson)

Many times a last time I will look
into this room like walking
fully clothed into a floodstream.
Under the candelabra in a hotel lobby or
on the train where the commuters ruffle
their papers, or standing in a corridor of
elevators, it will come before me
as though I could never leave.

When I came to you
like a woman who dressed herself in the morning,
who spread the fan of her hair
at night on your pillow, they were with us already,
those days we would live
out of what you had done alone.

You were the man of fear and omens
who cast his own death in the slant of a tree or
looking up, caused a star inside the head
to break from space, but more often
it was loss of the simplest talisman, expected,
a slight regret that could end all.

Mostly no one saw what was done. The dead
were unspectacular, scattered and inarticulate,
preferring to be handled and stepped over,
though at times they seemed to argue
among themselves, a continual racket about the beauty

of the universe or the piteousness of the human
voice, filling the ancient night
with their elaborate nostalgia.

Once there was no doubt. That one
was yours and you walked to him where he lay
and you took from his pockets
a picture, no wife or child, but an image of
himself. If he had raised up on one arm
and said in the language of the dying, 'Take this.
Remember me,' you would not have done less.
But no, the dead have no such rights and the living
are merciless, saying, 'Lie down. Be counted.'

Each day his eyes are opened on your wall
among the emblems that returned whole legions, no glad
survivors, but hostage to these harmless streets.
And I who did not see what was done
have seen him cut off at the neck, have heard him speak
full bodied. He is offended
there on your wall in his one death, in your one life.
He has changed his mind
and wants only to be forgotten, not entirely, no
just enough to surprise your continuing
pain. Pain that continues is not pain, outleaps

the body. That soldier
in the poster near the armchair
keeps running toward us extending his wing
of blood. It is too red. It is only the color
red. I have tried
to see it otherwise, but cannot.

You are right. What can I know, a woman
who was never there? Empathy, sad apron, I take you
on and off. In loving
it was the same. I almost
felt. Your pleasure was almost mine.

The white tree near the window
looks in on your bed, the flowered sheets
where I drift with the parachutes of the men
sinking into watery fields.
But what can I know? I
who may not be counted, womb
of your secret shame and silences:
companion, mourner, thief.

The Same Kiss After Many Years

Like a cat haunting the familiar porch,
it's found us again, we
who meet now only to hear
what didn't happen to us, but to them,
those two we sent away
into lives we wanted
to see happening to us.

They've done well for themselves, as
expected. He's an artist. His work
sells. She's aged, but well,
from her bones out, has
travel plans, time yet
to pick and choose.   ·

We're fond of them, not
just parental. Who else would listen
to us as we were
and take the blame
with such sad-eyed equanimity? They
know better now, would do it
over if they could.

We love their fateful hesitations,
self-caresses, the glance
that tells us plainly
there are those who await
their reappearance elsewhere. We're
concerned not to have them
missed, so this will happen
painlessly, leaving us all
the better for it.

They'll go back refreshed, seeing
how little we amounted to. Good
they got out when they did.
Let them kiss now, in the old
impassioned way, and go about their
business. They do it well, that
independence with a touch
of remorse. You're right. They're
better than we ever were. Kiss me.
Let's forget them.

Backdrop with Lovers, 1931

She's wearing a cotton dress
and sits on his lap casually, her arm
swung around his neck, as though she knew
this would happen, that moment, his hand
on her breast. Now we're all caught out here
in eternity by their expression in the singular.
Things were franker then?
Then. What may not be,
stopped.

Just as a quiver overtakes the landscape,
so each friendly beginning
is a hazard of sweet faces, birds flushed suddenly
from the lilac. Or because your manner
years later chooses an utter hopefulness,
we're made unequal
as the crowd parted by a blind walker. We
step aside and the calm planet of his head glides by.
That moment our thoughts stare
back at us, the nearest face closed
deeply into space.

She, then seventeen, could listen
while singing – her small wrists. Softly,
the important act takes place
without us, and she is crone now
or dead where painted treetops edge the blur
reminding. All that – years, back yards, sunning
in a neck-tied halter on the cellar door, whole cemeteries
of hopefulness have broken from sight
before the shutter. 'Hold still, hold it!' one voice
still trying to check our disappearance
between the makeshift stars. Behind them, the waves,
stylized, restless as party hats. Just looking
we are flying with multitudes
into their future, the open boat and backdrop
skimming into floodlights in the pines, where, where?
Your knowing not to ask.

My Mother Remembers That She Was Beautiful

(for Georgia Morris Bond)

The falling snow has made her thoughtful
and young in the privacy
of our table with its netted candle
and thick white plates. The serious faces
of the lights breathe on the pine boards
behind her. She is visiting
the daughter never close
or far enough away to come to.

She keeps her coat on, called into
her girlhood by such forgetting
I am gone or yet
to happen. She sees herself
among the townspeople, the country glances
slow with fields and sky
as she passes or waits
with a brother in the hot animal smell
of the auction stand: sunlight,
straw hats, a dog's tail
brushing her bare leg.

'There are things you know.
I didn't have to beg,' she said, 'for anything.'

The beautiful one speaks to me
from the changed, proud face and I see
how little I've let her know
of what she becomes. Years
were never the trouble, or the white hair
I braided near the sea
on a summer day. Who
she must have been
is lost to me through some fault
in my own reflection and we will have to go on
as we think we are, walking for no one's sake
from the empty restaurant into the one color
of the snow – before us, the close houses,
the brave and wondering lights of the houses.

FROM WILLINGLY
(1984)

Sudden Journey

Maybe I'm seven in the open field –
the straw grass so high
only the top of my head makes a curve
of brown in the yellow. Rain then.
First a little. A few drops on my
wrist, the right wrist. More rain.
My shoulders, my chin. Until I'm looking up
to let my eyes take the bliss.
I open my face. Let the teeth show. I
pull my shirt down past the collarbones.
I'm still a boy under my breast spots.
I can drink anywhere. The rain. My
skin shattering. Up suddenly, needing
to gulp, turning with my tongue, my arms out
running, running in the hard, cold plenitude
of all those who reach earth by falling.

Unsteady Yellow

I went to the field to break
and to bury my precious things.
I went to the field
with a sack and a spade,
to the cool field alone.

All that he gave me
I dashed and I covered.
The glass horse, the necklace,
the live bird with its song, with
its wings like two harps –
in the ground, in the damp ground.

Its song, when I snatched it again
to air, flung it with light
over the tall new corn, its pure joy
must have reached him.

In a day it was back, my freed bird
was back. Oh now, what will I do,
what will I do with its song
on my shoulder, with its heart
on my shoulder when we come to
the field, to the high yellow field?

Bird-Window-Flying

If we had been given names to love
each other by, I would take this one
from you, bird flying all day
in my woodhouse. The door
is open as when you came
to it, into it, as space between branches. 'Never
trust doors,' you tell the window,
the small of your body flung
against the white bay.

At dusk when I walked in
with my armload of green alder,
I could see the memory of light
shining water through your wings. You
were gray with it. The window
had aged you with promises.
I thought the boats, the gulls
should have stilled you
by now. When I cupped

my hands in their shadows, warm
over the heartwings, I saw the skin
of light between my fingers
haloed and glowing. Three steps I
took with you, for
you, three light years travelling
to your sky, beak
and claw of you, the soft burr of flight
at my fingerbones.

If I take a lover for every tree, I
will not have again such an opening as
when you flew from me.
I have gone in to build my fire. All
the walls, all the
wings of my house are burning. The flames
of me, the long hair
unbraiding.

I Save Your Coat, But You Lose It Later

It was a coat worth keeping even with
you in no condition to keep track, your mind
important to things you were seeing out
the window. We had changed seats on the bus
so a little breeze could catch
our faces. The coat was back there in a spot
of sunlight, its leather smell
making a halo of invitation around it.

We got off near the planetarium and were
heading for stars. Just to make one eye do
the work of two and bring back ghost-light
was making us forgetful. Then I looked at
you, strange without your coat, which
I knew you loved and had paid
an incredible price for, as if you had tried
to buy something that would make you sorry.

The bus was worrying itself into traffic, its
passengers locked into destinations. I ran
with everyone until they stopped in their
seats. There was your coat, a big interruption
in everybody's destination. When I picked it up,
it scalded my hand like an unbearable red
I saw once on a woman coming toward me.

We had a forty-year reunion right there
on the street, as if the coat
had met us again in its afterlife. We were

that glad, hugging it between us. Then you put
it on and checked yourself in the store window
wearing yourself those moments to see forgiveness
take your shape, then catching in the light
of those walking through you. I suppose it was
gratitude, your wearing it with telescopes, me
putting my hand in your pocket, pretending to
rob you while you looked for the first time
at the four moons of Jupiter.

Some weeks later, you write your coat was
stolen after a long night of drinking and
music. They took all your money. You never
saw it again. I am in a state of mourning
for your coat which travelled with us that while
like a close relative concealing a fatal illness
in a last visit. I remember a heart doctor
who saved a man for ten hours so his wife
disappeared into hope and would not come back
and would not take her lips from his until
they wheeled him away. I make too much of this,
your coat, which, stolen or lost, did not belong
to me, which I never wore.

The Hug

A woman is reading a poem on the street
and another woman stops to listen. We stop too,
with our arms around each other. The poem
is being read and listened to out here
in the open. Behind us
no one is entering or leaving the houses.

Suddenly a hug comes over me and I'm
giving it to you, like a variable star shooting light
off to make itself comfortable, then
subsiding. I finish but keep on holding
you. A man walks up to us and we know he hasn't
come out of nowhere, but if he could, he

would have. He looks homeless because of how
he needs. 'Can I have one of those?' he asks you,
and I feel you nod. I'm surprised,
surprised you don't tell him how
it is – that I'm yours, only
yours, etc., exclusive as a nose to
its face. Love – that's what we're talking about, love
that nabs you with 'for me
only' and holds on.

So I walk over to him and put my
arms around him and try to
hug him like I mean it. He's got an overcoat on
so thick I can't feel
him past it. I'm starting the hug
and thinking, 'How big a hug is this supposed to be?
How long shall I hold this hug?' Already
we could be eternal, his arms falling over my
shoulders, my hands not
meeting behind his back, he is so big!

I put my head into his chest and snuggle
in. I lean into him. I lean my blood and my wishes
into him. He stands for it. This is his
and he's starting to give it back so well I know he's
getting it. This hug. So truly, so tenderly
we stop having arms and I don't know if
my lover has walked away or what, or
if the woman is still reading the poem, or the houses –
what about them? – the houses.

Clearly, a little permission is a dangerous thing.
But when you hug someone you want it
to be a masterpiece of connection, the way the button
on his coat will leave the imprint of
a planet in my cheek
when I walk away. When I try to find some place
to go back to.

Devotion: That It Flow;
That There Be Concentration

I

My friend keeps kissing me goodbye, the kisses
landing, out of nervousness, on and about
the face. 'Leave the mistakes in,' Ives told
his conductor, handing him the new score.
So it feels good, these sudden lips jabbing the chin
and forehead. We couldn't repeat it if
we tried. Looking back to him from the train, I'll
wave, though not too long – like a soul heading into
the underworld – but more as one standing at
the beginning of the beginning, a faint
smile, or as with stage fright suffered inexplicably
in an orchard.
                    We're moving.
The card players in the club car look up
as though they could prevent countryside – but we're
slicing into marshland so surely, a river
gives way to hillside, the backs of houses, an iron
fence, the bricks of a factory where paper tubes
are made.
                Light falling into
            me. *Into*. Blades of light. Light
        with its own breath. So fast – the trees,
                            it moves the trees.

The porter has carried my suitcases.
Now he asks me how I want my coffee: 'Black,' I say,
'black and strong.'
'Like me,' he says, and it isn't a question.

It is mid-November and the first snow keeps arriving
between the tracks where the landscape stops briefly
at Providence. A bell rings. The iron wheels
shift for us. Snow, audible to the eyes, reconciles
endless variation. The tracks like a blank musical
score, running now beside us where the trees in clumps
dart up their sudden clefts.
                        Who's gone? Who's
            gone? Snowheart – where did you, into whose
                past go
            with only those particles of light
                        exactly melting?

I'm drinking coffee as we pass a child's camp –
a hatch of discarded boards. It is perched
like the abandoned nest of some enormous bird,
topping a bluff which carries as memory
into childhood where once we dug a house into
a hillside. The smell of earth fresh around us, dirt
sifting out of our sleeves beside our plates
at supper. We were the dead children, come home
to sit in goodness with the silence of our ghostly
parents. Now we are gone, and so are they, and where
I look up, the child's camp is a thicket the snow
has breathed on.

Vision shaved away – the cords of my vision
electric, sparked in the current of
fast ditches, fast silos, chimneys that leap and
dodge the banks. Water
standing in yellow grass, leaves, a few
left hanging, tortured so
the words *defoliation* and *napalm* occur.

The opening pages of Malraux's *Lazarus*: mustard gas
drifting over the Russians in their trenches at Bolgako
until the Germans change their minds about killing
those they have already killed, take the dead
and half-living soldiers in their arms and
stumble back to lives never again the same.

Passing as another kind of dwelling.
At night the mills are torches between
the trees. The snow climbs up, floats
under the blue
dark. The tunnels
of the rabbits quiver and loosen when
the fur rushes through them.

II

I have travelled like sky with water far below, an
interlocking of surfaces. Or does the water lift
when sky hints into infinity
that change is the only durable ghost? This powder
of moments sheds the difference. Each shift,
eccentric and willful, is recorded as surely as
the chambers of the heart record blood
that will pass again, asking from time to
time where the body is.

Interior of my face in the window, axis
    with a darkening motion.
        The mind flies out
            into this unconcealing.
                Shadows
                    I kissed.
  The rutted track of thought without
                purpose.

We arrive at Mystic, the mind feeling itself as surface
to steeple, lumberyard, old barrels, a newly built
set of steps heading for a second story: 'Up!'
my sight says, until a door opens
          and a child steps out
                    onto the landing.

III

We pass over trains, then into a conflicting mesh
of wrecked machines. A gull appears like a fish
above an empty playground. Then *WALL*, its rushing: *WALL*
inches from my window, the eyes – their flesh
driven back into the body.

How many times we defy matter heading into the ground
until it rises to either side – shoots by as motion
suddenly delivered to hillside or the mind incarnate –
retaining each recent death at its most living point.

Lunch at Old Saybrook.
The elderly woman across from me reads her newspaper
with a magnifying glass. Something blue flashes by.
        Blue catches
in the landscape for miles.

The woman has spread her coat across her knees.
She is asleep, or seems so. A graveyard near a river
startles no one's composure, though some
who didn't mean to be looking must see it, where,
in its stead, a yellow truck passes to a yellow house
we lose before woods again.

The woman is asleep and I think my seeing keeps
the world for her. I think of her
like a picnic table in winter, passively unanchored
by the season. I see IS
under her magnifying glass in the empty seat next to her.

IV

At night the houses flicker
between the trees. Every light is the same face you
cannot leave, saying: 'I am not leaving,
though I kiss the last mouth, yours, even
yours, without touching.'

My eye roars its black blood across the snow-light. My
lantern swings me in a golden arc.
Show-me-show-me: the dwarf flowers
of their heads
in the windows, in the night water.

Bless now
each lit place where no one
will pass tonight, these yellow shrines, elbows
into the dark.

V

The porter wants to know what I've written.
I read it to him where he stands in the aisle, and
he says, 'That's beautiful. Is that
what you do for a living?'
'Yes,' I say, 'for a living.'

We pull into yet another station, and he pats my hand,
leans close. 'You're lucky,' he says, and I feel
all that has gotten away from me
in what he misses. When I step down
onto the platform, there is a train in my memory.
Memory which rushes to add itself
to the startling impression of future pouring in.

The sleeping woman stays with the train, sleeping on,
grave and constant as the silent towns arrive.

Not There

One whistle, a short husky breath —
like a child blowing into a metal pipe then
listening. The house shudders
as the train passes on the hillside.
Days, mornings — whatever I'm doing I stop
and rush to wave it by. But always
I'm too late for the engineer.
It's the man in the caboose
who's searched out my doorway.
His grave face and hand say *hello-goodbye*.

Other times the train is coming
and I don't go out. I go on
doing what I'm doing — reading, or staring
at the gulls rising and falling above
the waves. I don't
go out. A weight pulls
against the house. I think of his grave face
looking down at the house, of the woman
in the doorway. I don't go out and
I don't go out. These
are the moments when we meet.

Crêpes Flambeau

We are three women eating out
in a place that could be California
or New Jersey but is Texas and our waiter
says his name is Jerry. He is pink
and young, dressed in soft denim
with an embroidered vest and, my friend says,
a nice butt. It's hard not to be intimate
in America where your waiter wants
you to call him Jerry. So why
do you feel sorry for him
standing over the flames
of this dessert?

The little fans of the crêpes are
folding into the juice. The brandy
is aflare in a low blue hush and golden
now and red where he spills
the brown sugar saved
to make our faces wear the sudden burst. We
are all good-looking and older and he
has to please us or try
to. What could go wrong? Too much
brandy? Too little sugar? Fire
falling into our laps, fire
like laughter behind his back, even
when he has done it just right. 'Jerry,'
we say, 'that was wonderful,' for now
he is blushing at us
like a russet young girl. Our lips

are red with fire and juice.
He knows we could go on
eating long into the night until the flames
run down our throats. 'Thank you,'
he says, handing us our check, knowing
among the ferns and napkins that he has
pleased us, briefly, like all
good things, dying away
at the only moment, before
we are too happy, too
glad in the pioneer decor: rough boards,
spotted horses in the frame.

Conversation with a Fireman from Brooklyn

He offers, between planes,
to buy me a drink. I've never talked
to a fireman before, not one from Brooklyn
anyway. Okay. Fine, I say. Somehow
the subject is bound to come up, women
firefighters, and since I'm
a woman and he's a fireman, between
the two of us, we know something
about this subject. Already

he's telling me he doesn't mind
women firefighters, but what
they look like
after fighting a fire, well
they lose all respect. He's sorry, but
he looks at them
covered with the cinders of someone's
lost hope, and he feels disgust, he just
wants to turn the hose on them, they
are that sweaty and stinking, just like
him, of course, but not the woman he
wants, you get me? and to come to that –
isn't it too bad, to be despised
for what you do to prove yourself
among men
who want to love you, to love you,
love you.

Some with Wings, Some with Manes

Over the stone wall her hand comes,
each knuckle enlarged to a miniature
skull. She reaches into my rented yard
to call me neighbor. Sunlight dazzles
her spectacles, and in the chromium glint
of her walker she is bright royalty
on an errand of magnitude. An effort to
stand, an effort to step the pain
carefully around invisible parameters
and still to say: effort is nobility.

Her hands are perfectly good for pointing.
That small, bare tree near my walkway, if
pruned, would be heavy with peaches
the size of your fist by July. In new regard,
I think what it could and will do. Then, not
to demean its offering, keep the next thought –
that I'll be gone by summer.

She has the name of a workhorse
I knew in Missouri, Dolly, and has outlived
a sister lost to the same disease. 'She
sat down with it and that was the end of
her.' Such variations on reluctance
cause me to see a kite
stubborn in a childhood pear tree, still abash
in the wind with its complication
of branches. I sighted my days
by its banners, until the tree caressed
it into flight, one day I wasn't looking.

For didn't the memory of the tree go with
it, the shred of it, less articulate
by then, a slip of motion longing to wrap itself
in a tattered lunge at the whole air?
After that, the tree said only the same thing
other trees say before coming to fruit.
Somehow we knew in our child-hearts
when a thing is ruined, not to meddle
with ecstasy by setting it free. We left it,
though it ruffles the mind yet.

Sitting in the darkened afternoon of her
living room, I hear the death
of the only daughter, meet the husband
who loves eggs and sweets, says little.
'I'm the last of my family,' she says, then,
in the walker, leads me down the grassy corridor
to a room sleeping like a princess. The spell,
I see, is in the elaborate coverlet.

She will teach me how to do it. 'It
took me fourteen months of evenings,'
the hands now going out
to the stitched pieces, remembering they
have done this. I know I will never do it,
will be gone by summer. 'What is it called?'
'Cathedral Windows,' she says,
and the razed light of her hands
falls over me.

View from an Empty Chair

Late afternoon light between peach trees.
No movement. Just one child-voice
telling another, 'I'll show you!' – then
heading into valor – sound of furious pedaling,
clash of spokes. A wash of sparrows
breathes from a rooftop where periscopes
of pipes and ducts cause the houses
to submerge in the deep air.

Behind me, the muzzle of a hound
snuffles the stone ledge. Mournfully, I
occur to him, an intonation of wrongness
in the landscape. I feel the danger I mean
to someone unknown and near.

Over the wall a coffee mug appears, then
upper torso. The woman lets the dog
bound against her. 'He hates
men,' she tells me. His soft, loose mouth
lunges against the guard-wire – proving
loyalty by insistence on threat.

She lives alone, has had tools
stolen from the patio. Visitors and
burglars chance the house dog, a terrier
I hear as *terror*. (The air
is finely tuned.) One glance away
and her head is gone.

Country western bleeds from a doorway
opened brightly to *there goes my
everything*, then shut so birds
come in as underscoring to a car
luffing past. My house, with quiet skill,
intends to pull over me
with shadow.

The child recurs, imitating death pains
as comic and reversible. Taking up
my sweater and waterglass, I catch hold
of a child's drawing the wind has carried
into the yard. It has a friendly aspect,
the mouth like a hammock, though the hands

are levers and the eyes – demented
and aslant. We brighten once before
the house drops over us.

[El Paso, 1979]

Tableau Vivant

They think it's easy to be dead, those
who walk the pathway here in stylish shoes,
portable radios strapped to their arms,
selling the world's perishables, even
love songs. They think you just lie down
into dreams you will never tell anyone
They don't know we still have plans, a yen
for romance, and miss things like hats
and casseroles.

As for dreams, we take up where the living
leave off. We like especially those
in which the dreamer is about to
fall over a cliff or from a bridge that
is falling too. We're only too glad
to look down on the river gorge enlarging
under a body's sudden weight, to have the ground
rushing up instead of this slow
caving in. We thrive on living out
the last precious memories of someone escaped
back into morning light.

Occasionally there's a message saying they want
one of us back, someone out there
feeling guilty about a word or deed
that seems worse because we took it as
a living harm, then died
with it, quietly. But we know a lot about
forgiveness and we always make these trips with
a certain missionary zeal. We get back
into our old sad clothes. We stand again
at the parting, full of wronged tenderness and
needing a shave or a hairdo. We tell them
things are okay, not to waste their lives
in remorse, we never held it
against them, so much happens that no one means.

But sometimes one of us gets stubborn, thinks
of evening the score. We leave them calling
after us, *Sorry, Sorry, Sorry*, and we don't
look back.

Reading Aloud
(for David Delaittre)

When the light was shutting down on you
I said, 'Behind my home is a palace of mountains.'
I wanted you to see them, regal
in their shawls of snow above the working houses
of the town. I told them to you
the way a mother tells death to a child, so it seems
possible to go there and stay, leaving everyone
behind, saying softly, 'Everyone's coming,'
so it's only a little while alone.

You were slipping from our days
like an opposite ripeness, still clinging
to the light. Each time you guessed your way home
by the edges, I saw my own image
freed in the streets of your memory, my face
like a time traveller's, forever young,
and every place you touched gave way.

I called it my year of the blind.
I was working for your friend who lived
a blindness he was born to.
'What did he lose? Noises, that's all
he knows,' you said, would have no comfort
or instruction.

Long days I read aloud to your friend
the words that are the fountain sounds of the mind
causing light to fall inside itself over
the missing shapes of the world. 'What do you think
when I say "wings"?' I asked once. 'Angels,
birds,' he said, and I saw he could fly
with either. Once, about diamonds,
'Their light – a hiss in the rain
when the cars pass.'

But you were memory-taunted by what was left
of your sight – the face of a beautiful
grade school teacher marooned in your childhood.
You cried against her neck and were grown.

The day we set out for the mountains
I strapped your sleeping bag to your back.
The woman who would call you 'husband'
bound up her long hair and said your name
each time you fell and got up, *David, David.*
When we came to the chasm where a moss-slick log
was the only bridge, we looked down for you
at the river stones, the water over
and over them.

She loved you too much and could not lead you.
I took your hand and put all my sight there,
balancing between trust and the swiftness
we could fall to, walking backwards
so my grip was steady. When the river-sound
rocked us to either side, I fell deeper
for how you gave up to me
and to the river where we walked
like two improbable Christs held up by the doubt
that is the body.
When I let your hand drop on the far side
and we sank in the earth, the habit
of thanks was in me. Who could go with us
after that, though they joined us?

When I think of you in the years that have
passed us, I see a river under you
and always you are walking
into the shouting light of water and again
the wet smell of cloth
as when someone has been lifted free
with their breath still in them.

I know your walking is the other side of courage
and has no regard, like the cold faces
of the mountains seen from a childhood window
when the house is empty, when
with our many hands we have rushed through the rooms,
adding darkness, adding the words *mother, father,*
and no one answers back.

From Dread in the Eyes of Horses

Eggs. Dates and camel's milk.
Give this. In one hour the foal will
stand, in two will run. The care then of
women, the schooling from fear, clamor
of household, a prospect of saddles.

They kneel to it, folded
on its four perfect legs, stroke
the good back, the muscles bunched at the chest.
Its head, how the will shines large in it
as what may be used to overcome it.

The women of the horses comb out
their cruel histories of hair only for
the pleasure of horses, for the lost mares
on the Ridge of Yellow Horses, their white arms
praying the hair down breasts ordinary

as knees. The extent of their power,
this intimation of sexual wealth. From dread
in the eyes of horses are taken their songs.
In the white forests the last free horses
eat branches and roots, are hunted like deer
and carry no one.

A wedge of light where the doorway opens
the room – in it, a sickness of sleep.
The arms of the women, their coarse
white hair. In a bank of sunlight, a man
whitewashes the house he owns – no shores, no
worlds above it and farther, shrill, obsidian,
the high feasting of the horses.

Death of the Horses by Fire

We have seen a house in the sleeping town
stand still for a fire and the others,
where their windows knew it,
clothed in the remnants of a dream
happening outside them. We have seen
the one door aflame in the many windows,
the steady procession of the houses
trembling in heat-light, their well-tended
yards, the trellis of cabbage roses scrawled
against the porch – flickering white, whiter
where a darkness breathes back.

How many nights the houses have burned through
to morning. We stood in our blankets
like a tribe made to witness
what a god could do.

We saw the house built again in daylight
and children coming from it
as what a house restores to itself in rooms
so bright they do not forget, even
when the father, when the mother
dies. 'Kitchen of your childhoods!' we shout
at the old men alive on the benches
in the square. Their good, black eyes
glitter back at us, a star-fall
of homecomings.

Only when the horses began to burn
in the funnel of light hurrying in one place
on the prairie did we begin to suspect
our houses, to doubt at our meals
and pleasures. We gathered on the ridge
above the horses, above the blue smoke
of the grasses, and they whirled in the close
circle of the death that came to them, rippling in
like a deep moon to its water. With
the hills in all directions
they stood in the last of their skies
and called to each other to save them.

3 A.M. Kitchen: My Father Talking

For years it was land working me, oil fields,
cotton fields, then I got some land. I
worked it. Them days you could just about
make a living. I was logging.

Then I sent to Missouri. Momma
come out. We got married.
We got some kids. Five kids.
That kept us going.

We bought some land near the water.
It was cheap then. The water
was right there. You just looked out
the window. It never left the window.

I bought a boat. Fourteen footer.
There was fish out there then.
You remember, we used to catch
six, eight fish, clean them right
out in the yard. I could of fished to China.

I quit the woods. One day just
walked out, took off my corks, said that's
it. I went to the docks.
I was driving winch. You had to watch
to see nothing fell out of the sling. If
you killed somebody you'd
never forget it. All
those years I was just working
I was on edge, every day. Just working.

You kids. I could tell you
a lot. But I won't.

It's winter. I play a lot of cards
down at the tavern. Your mother.
I have to think of excuses
to get out of the house. You're
wasting your time, she says. You're wasting
your money.

You don't have no idea, Threasie.
I run out of things
to work for. Hell, why shouldn't I
play cards? Threasie,
some days now I just don't know.

Boat Ride

(for Galway)

Since my girlhood, in that small boat
we had gone together for salmon
with the town still sleeping and the wake
a white groove in the black water, black
as it is when the gulls are just stirring and
the ships in the harbor are sparked with lights
like the casinos of Lucerne.
That morning my friend had driven an hour
in darkness to go with us, my father
and me. There'd been an all-night party.
My friend's face so tired I thought, *Eskimo-eyes.*
He sighed, as if stretched out
on a couch at the back of his mind.

Getting the bait and tackle. What
about breakfast? No breakfast.
Bad luck to eat breakfast before fishing, but
good luck to take smoked salmon to eat
on the water in full sun. Was my friend's coat
warm enough? The wind can come up.
Loaning him my brother's plaid jacket.

Being early on the water, like getting first
to heaven and looking back through memory
and longing at the town. Talking little, and
with the low, tender part
of our voices; not sentences but
friendlier, as in nodding to one who already
knows what you mean.

Father in his rain-slicker – seaweed green over
his coat, over blue work shirt, over cream-
colored thermal underwear that makes a white V

at his neck. His mouth open so the breath
doesn't know if it's coming or going – like any
other wave without a shore. His mind
in the no-thought of guiding the boat.
I stare into the water folding
along the bow, *gentian* – the blue with darkness
engraved into its name, so the sound
petals open with mystery.

Motor-sound, a low burbling with a chuckle
revolving in the *smack smack* of the bow
spanking water. *You hear me, but you don't
hear me*, the motor says
to the fish. A few stars
over the mountains above the town.
I think *pigtails*, and that the water under us
is at least as high as those mountains, deep
as the word *cello* whispered under water –
cello, cello until it frees a greeting.

We pass the Coast Guard station, its tower
flashing cranky white lights beside
the barracks where the seamen sleep in
long rows. Past the buoy, its sullen red bell
tilting above water. All this time
without fishing – important to get out of
the harbor before letting the lines
down, not time wasted but time
preparing, which includes invitation and
forgetting, so the self is occupied freely
in idleness.

'Just a boat ride,' my father says, squinting
where sun has edged the sky toward Dungeness
a hazy mix of violet and pink. 'Boat ride?'
I say. 'But we want salmon.'
'I'll take cod, halibut, old shoes, anything
that's going,' says my friend. 'And you'll get
dogfish,' my father says. 'There's enough
dogfish down there to feed all Japan.'
He's baiting up, pushing the double hooks
through the herring. He watches us
let the lines out. 'That's plenty,' he says,
like it's plain this won't come
to much.

Sitting then, nothing to say for a while,
poles nodding slightly. My friend, slipping
a little toward sleep, closes his eyes.
Car lights easing along Ediz Hook, some
movement in the town, Port of the Angels,
the angels turning on kitchen lights,
wood smoke stumbling among scattered hemlock,
burning up questions, the angels telling
their children to get up, planning the future
that is one day long.

'Hand me that coffee bottle, Sis,' my father
says. 'Cup of coffee always makes the fish
bite.' Sure enough, as he lifts the cup,
my pole hesitates, then dips. I brace
and reel. 'Damned dogfish!' my father says,
throwing his cigarette into the water. 'How
does he know?' my friend asks. 'No fight,'
I say. 'They swallow the hook down
their gullets. You have to cut
the leader.'

No sun-flash on silver scales when it
breaks water, but thin-bellied brown, shark-
like, and the yellow-eyed insignia
that says: *there will be more of us.*
Dogfish. Swallower of hooks, waster of hopes
and tackle. My father grabs the line, yanks
the fish toward the knife, slashes twice,
gashing the throat and underbelly so
the blood spills over his hand.
'There's one that won't come back,' he says.

My friend witnesses without comment or
judgment the death and mutilation
of the dogfish. The sun is up. My friend
is wide awake now. We are all wide
awake. The dogfish floats away, and a tenderness
for my father wells up in me, my father
whom I want my friend to love and who intends,
if he must, as he will, to humor us, to keep
fishing, to be recorded in the annals
of dogfish as a scourge on the nation of
dogfish which has fouled his line, which is
unworthy and which he will single-handedly
wipe out.

When the next fish hits my friend's line
and the reel won't sing, I take out my
Instamatic camera: 'That's a beautiful
dogfish!' I say. 'I'll tell them in New York
it's a marlin,' my friend says. I snap
his picture, the fish held like
a trophy. My father leans out of
the frame, then cuts the line.

In a lull I get him to tell stories,
the one where he's a coal miner in Ottumwa,
Iowa, during the Depression and the boss
tries to send the men into a mine where
a shaft collapsed the day before. 'You'll
go down there or I'll run you out of
this town,' the boss says. 'You don't
have to run me. I'm not just leaving
your town, I'm leaving your whole goddamned
state!' my father says, and he turns
and heads on foot out of the town, some
of the miners with him, hitching from there
to the next work in the next state.

My father knows he was free
back there in 1935 in Ottumwa, Iowa, and he
means you to know you don't have to risk
your life for pay if you can tell the boss to
go to hell and turn your heel. What
he doesn't tell is thirty years on the docks,
not a day missed – working, raising
a family.

I unwrap smoked salmon sandwiches and we bite
into them. It is the last fishing trip
I will have with my father. He
is ready to tell the one about the time
he nearly robbed the Seminole Bank in
Seminole, Oklahoma, but got drunk
instead and fell asleep.
He is going to kill five more dogfish
without remorse; and I am going to
carry a chair outside for him
onto the lawn of the Evergreen Radiation
Center where he will sit and smoke
and neither of us feels like talking, just
his – 'The sun feels good.'

After treatments, after going back
to my sister's where he plays with her baby –
'There's my gal! Is the Kiss Bank
open?' – in the night, rising up in the dream
of his going to say, 'Get my billfold,' as if
even his belongings might be pulled into
the vortex of what would come.

We won't catch a single salmon that day.
No strikes even. My friend and I
will share a beer and reminisce in advance
about the wonderful dogfishing we had.
My father wipes blood from his knife
across his knee and doesn't
look up. He believes nothing
will survive of his spirit or body. His god
takes everything and will not be
satisfied, will not be assuaged by the hopes, by
the pitiful half-measures of the living.
If he is remembered, that too
will pass.

It is good then,
to eat salmon on the water, to bait the hook
again, even for dogfish, to stare back at
the shore as one who withholds nothing, who,
in the last of himself, cannot put together
that meaning, and need not, but yields in thought
so peacefully to the stubborn brightness of
light and water: we are awake with him
as if we lay asleep. Good memory,
if you are such a boat, tell me
we did not falter in the vastness
when we walked ashore.

Accomplishment

(for my father, Leslie Bond, 1909-1982)

What not to do for him
was hardest, for the life left in us
argued against his going
like a moon banished in fullness, yet
lingering far into morning, pale
with new light, gradually a view of
mountains, a sea emerging – its prickly
channels and dark shelves
breeding in the violet morning. Ships too,
after a while. Some anchored, others
moving by degree, as if to leave without affront
this harbor, a thin shoal curved like an arm –
ever embracing, ever releasing.

He too was shaped to agreement, the hands
no longer able to hold, at rest
on the handmade coverlet. His tongue
arched forward in the open mouth where breath
on breath he labored, the task beyond all strength
so the body shuddered like a chill
on the hinge of his effort, then rose again.

After a time, we saw the eyes gaze upward
without appeal – eyes without knowing or need
of knowing. Some in the room began to
plead, as if he meant to take them with him,
and they were afraid. A daughter bent near,
calling his name, then gave her own,
firmly, like a dock he might swim or cling to.
The breath eased, then drifted momentarily,
considering or choosing, we did not know.

'At some point we have to let him go.'
'I know,' she said. 'I know.'

In the last moments the eyes widened and,
with the little strength left, he
strained upward and toward. 'He had to be
looking *at* something. You don't look
at *nothing* that way.' Not
pain, but some sharpening beyond
the visible. Not eagerness or surprise, but

as though he would die in time to intercept
an onrushing world, for which
he had prepared himself
with that dead face.

Black Silk

She was cleaning – there is always
that to do – when she found,
at the top of the closet, his old
silk vest. She called me
to look at it, unrolling it carefully
like something live
might fall out. Then we spread it
on the kitchen table and smoothed
the wrinkles down, making our hands
heavy until its shape against Formica
came back and the little tips
that would have pointed to his pockets
lay flat. The buttons were all there.
I held my arms out and she
looped the wide armholes over
them. 'That's one thing I never
wanted to be,' she said, 'a man.'
I went into the bathroom to see
how I looked in the sheen and
sadness. Wind chimes
off-key in the alcove. Then her
crying so I stood back in the sink-light
where the porcelain had been staring. Time
to go to her, I thought, with that
other mind, and stood still.

Candle, Lamp & Firefly

How can I think what thoughts
to have of you with a mind so unready?
What I remember most: you did not want
to go. Then choice slipped from you
like snow from the mountain, so death
could graze you over with the sweet
muzzles of the deer moving up from
the valleys, pausing to stare
down and back toward the town. But you
did not gaze back. Like a cut rose
on the fifth day, you bowed
into yourself and we watched the shell-
shaped petals drop in clumps, then,
like wine, deepen into the white cloth.

What have you written here on my sleep
with flesh so sure I have no choice
but to stare back when your face and
gestures follow me into daylight?
Your arms, too weak at your death
for embracing, closed around me and held,
and such a tenderness was mixed there
with longing that I asked, 'Is it good
where you are?'

We echoed a long time in the kiss
that was drinking me – *daughter, daughter,
daughter* – until I was gone as when a sun
drops over the rim of an ocean, gone
yet still there. Then the dampness,
the chill of your body pulled from me
into that space the condemned
look back to after parting.

Between sleep and death
I carry no proof that we met, no proof
but to tell what even I must call dream
and gently dismiss. So does
a bird dismiss one tree for another
and carries each time the flight between
like a thing never done.

And what is proof then, but some trance
to kill the birds? And what are dreams
when the eyes open on similar worlds
and you are dead in my living?

Woodcutting on Lost Mountain

(for Leslie and for Morris)

Our father is three months dead
from lung cancer and you light another Camel,
ease the chainsaw into the log. You
don't need habits to tell us
you're the one most like him.
Maybe the least loved
carries injury farther into tenderness
for having first to pass through
forgiveness. You
passed through. 'I think he respected me
at the end,' as if you'd waited a lifetime
to offer yourself that in my listening.

'Top of the mountain!' your daughter cries.
She's ten, taking swigs with us
from the beer can in the January sun. We see
other mountain tops and trees forever.
A mountain *could* get lost in all this, right
enough, even standing on it, thinking this
is where you are.

'Remember the cabins we built when we were
kids? The folks logging Deer Park and
Black Diamond.' My brother, Morris, nods,
pulls the nose of the saw into the air as a chunk
falls. 'We built one good one. They
brought their lunches and sat with us
inside – Spam sandwiches on white bread,
bananas for dessert and Mountain Bars, white
on the inside, pure sugar on
the inside – the way they hurt your teeth.'

Sawdust sprays across his knee, his face
closes in thought. 'Those whippings.' He
cuts the motor, wipes his forehead with an arm.
'They'd have him in jail today. I used to beg
and run circles. You got it worse because you
never cried. It's a wonder we didn't
run away.' 'Away to where?' I say. 'There's no
away when you're a kid. Before you can get there
you're home.'

'Once he took you fishing and left me
behind,' my brother says.
'I drew pictures of you sinking
all over the chicken house. I gave you a head
but no arms. We
could go back today and there
they'd be, boats
sinking all down the walls.'

His daughter is Leslie, named after our father.
Then I think – 'She's a logger's daughter,
just like me' – and the thought pleases as if
the past had intended this present. 'You
didn't know you were doing it,' I tell him,
'but you figured how to stay
in our childhood.' 'I guess I did. There's
nothing I'd rather do,' he says, 'than cut wood.
Look at that –' he points to stacks of logs
high as a house he's thinned from the timber –
'they're going to burn them. Afraid
somebody might take a good tree
for firewood, so they'll burn half a forest.
Damn, that's the Forest Service for you. Me –
I work here, they'll have to stop me.'

Leslie carries split wood to the tailgate
and I toss it into the truck. We make
a game of it, trying to stack as fast
as her father cuts. 'She's a worker,'
Morris says. 'Look at that girl go.
Sonofagun, I wouldn't trade four boys for her.
No sir.' He picks up the maul, gives a yell
and whacks down through the center of a block
thick as a man. It falls neatly into
halves. 'Look at that! Now *that's* good wood.
That's beautiful wood,' he says, like he
made it himself.

I tell him how the cells of trees
are like the blood cells of people, how trees
are the oldest organisms on the earth. Before
the English cut the trees off Ireland, the Irish
had three dozen words for green. He's impressed,
mildly, has his own way of thinking about trees.

Tomorrow a log pile will collapse
on him and he will just get out alive.

'Remember the time Dad felled the tree on us
and Momma saved us, pushed us into a ditch? It's
a wonder we ever grew up.'

'One of the horses they logged with, Dick
was his name, Old Dick. They gave him
to Oney Brown and Dick got into the house
while everyone was gone and broke
all the dishes. Dishes – what could they mean
to a horse? Still, I think he knew
what he was doing.'

Oney's wife, Sarah, had fifteen kids. She's
the prettiest woman I'll ever see. Her son,
Lloyd, took me down to the railroad tracks
to show me the dead hounds. 'We had too many
so they had to shoot some.' The hounds were
skeletons by then, but they haven't moved
all these years from the memory
of that dark underneath of boughs.
I look at them, stretched on their sides, twin
arches of bones leaping with beetles and
crawlers into the bark-rich earth. Skipper
and Captain – Cappy for short. Their names
and what seemed incomprehensible – a betrayal
which meant those who had care of you
might, without warning, make an end of you
in some godforsaken, heartless place. Lloyd spat
like a father between the tracks, took
my hand and led me back to the others.

Twenty years settles on the boys
of my childhood. Some of them loggers.
'It's gone,' they tell me. 'The Boom Days
are gone. We thought
they'd never end, there were
that many trees. But it's finished,
or nearly. Nothing but stumps
and fireweed now.'

'Alaska,' Morris says, 'that's where the trees
are,' and I think of them, like some lost tribe
of wanderers, their spires and bloodless blood
climbing cathedral-high into the moss-light
of days on all the lost mountains of
our childhoods.

Coming into the town we see the blue smoke
of the trees streaming like a mystery
the houses hold in common.
'Doesn't seem possible – ,' he says, 'a tree
nothing but a haze you could
put your hand through.'

'What'll you do next, after the trees are gone?'

'Pack dudes in for elk.'

'Then what?'

'Die, I guess. Hell, I don't know, ask
a shoemaker, ask a salmon…
Remember that time I was hunting and got lost,
forgot about the dark and me with no coat, no
compass? You and Dad fired rifles from the road
until I stumbled out. It
was midnight. But I got out. It's a wonder
I could tell an echo from a shot, I was so cold,
so lost. Stop cussing, I told the old man, I'm
home, ain't I? "You're grown," he kept saying,
"you're a grown man."
I must be part wild. I must be part tree or part
deer. I got on the track and I was lost
but it didn't matter. I had to go where it led.
I must be part bobcat.'

Leslie is curled under my arm, asleep.

'Truck rocks them to sleep,' Morris says.
'Reminds me, I don't have a license for this
piece of junk. I hope I don't get stopped. Look
at her sleep! right in the middle of the day.
Watch this: "Wake up honey, we're lost. Help me
get home. You went to sleep and got us lost."
She must be part butterfly, just look at those eyes.
There – she's gone again. I'll have to carry
her into the house. Happens every time.

Watch her, we'll go up the steps and she'll be
wide awake the minute I open the door.
Hard to believe, we had to be carried into houses
once, you and me. It's a wonder we ever
grew up.'

Tomorrow a log pile will collapse
and he'll just get out alive.

He opens the door. Her eyes start,
suddenly awake.

'See, what'd I tell you. Wide awake. Butterfly,
you nearly got us lost, sleeping so long.
Here, walk for yourself. We're home.'

Some Painful Butterflies Pass Through

I saw the old Chinese men standing
in Nanjing under the trees where
they had hung their caged birds
in the early morning, as though a cage
were only another branch that travels
with us. The bird revolves and settles,
moving its mind up and down the tree
with leaves and light. It sings
with the free birds – what else
can it do? They sit on the rungs
and preen or jit back and down and
back. But they are busy
and a day in the sky makes wings
of them. Then some painful butterflies
pass through.

The old men talk and smoke, examine
each other's cages. They feel restored,
as if they'd given themselves a tree, a sky
full of companions, song
that can travel. They depend
on their birds, and if their love stories
swing from their arms as they walk
homeward, it may be they are chosen
after all like one tree
with one bird that is faithful,
an injured voice travelling high into silence
with one accustomed listener
who smiles and walks slowly with
his face in the distance so
the pleasure spreads, and the treasured
singing, and the little bursts
of flying.

[Shanghai, 11 June 1983]

Gray Eyes

When she speaks it is like coming onto a grave
    at the edge of a woods, softly, so we
        do not enter or wholly
     turn away. Such speech
  is the breath a brush makes through hair,
      opening into time
    after the stroke.

      A tree is bending
but the bird doesn't land.

    One star,
earthbound, reports a multitude of unyielding
  others. It
     cannot help its   falling   falling
into the dull brown earth of someone's back yard,
  where, in daylight, a hand reaches
in front of the mower and tosses it, dead stone,
       aside. We who saw it fall

are still crashing with light into the housetops,
  tracing in the mind that missing
     trajectory, rainbow of darkness
  where we were – children
murmuring – 'There, over there!' – while the houses
  slept and slept on.

Years later she is still nesting on the light
  of that plundered moment, her black hair
    frozen to her head with yearning,
  saying, 'Father, I am a colder green
    where the mower cut a swath
     and I lay down
and the birds that have no use for song
    passed over me
  like a shovel-fall.'

She closed her eyes. It was early morning. Daybreak.
  Some bees
       were dying on my wing – humming
   so you could hardly hear.

Linoleum

(for Mark Strand)

There are the few we hear of
like Christ, who, with divine grace,
made goodness look easy, had
a following to draw near, gave up
the right things and saw to it
that sinners got listened to.
Sharpening my failures, I remember
the Jains, the gentle swoosh
of their brooms on a dirt path
trodden by children and goats, each
thoughtful step taken in peril of
an ant's life or a fat grub hidden
under a stick. In the car wash,
thinking of yogis under a tree
plucking hair by hair the head
of an initiate, I feel at least
elsewhere those able for holiness –
its signs and rigors – are at work.
Ignominiously, I am here, brushes
clamped, soap and water pulsing
against my car. (A good sign too,
those asylums for old and diseased
animals.) My car is clean
and no one has had to
lift a finger. The dead
bugs have been gushed away into a soup
of grit and foam – the evidence
not subterranean, but streaming along
the asphalt in sunlight so dazzling
I attend the birth-moment of
the word *Hosannah!*

I care about the bugs and not
in this life will I do enough towards
my own worth in the memory
of them. I appreciate the Jains,
their atonements for my neglect,
though I understand it makes poor farmers
of them, and good we all
don't aspire to such purity so
there's somebody heartless enough to
plow the spuds.

Early on, in admiration, I put off
knowledge, and so delayed reading about
the Jains – not to lose
solace. But in the county library,
turning a page, I meet them as
the wealthiest moneylenders
in Western India. Reading on,
I'm encouraged – the list of virtues
exceeds vices – just four
of those: anger, pride, illusion and
greed. The emphasis clearly on
striving. I write them down
in the corner of a map
of Idaho: forbearance, indulgence,
straightforwardness, purity,
veracity, restraint, freedom from
attachment to anything, poverty
and chastity.

Choosing, getting into the car to
get to the supermarket, hearing
over engine noise the bright agonies
of birds, the radio news with the child
nailed into a broom closet for
twenty-four hours by parents who
in straightforwardness sacrificed
forbearance, I feel a longing
for religion, for doctrine swift
as a broom to keep the path
clear. Later, alone in the kitchen
with the groceries, I read the list
again. Overwhelmed by the loneliness
of the saints, I take up my broom
and begin where I stand,
with linoleum.

Willingly

When I get up he has been long at work,
his brush limber against the house.
Seeing him on his ladder under the eaves,
I look back on myself asleep in the dream
I could not carry awake. Sleep
inside a house that is being painted,
whole lifetimes now only the familiar cast
of morning light over the prayer plant.
This 'not remembering' is something new
of where you have been.

What was settled or unsettled in sleep
stays there. But your house   .
under his steady arm is leaving itself
and you see this gradual surface of
new light covering your sleep
has the greater power.
You think now you felt brush strokes or
the space between them, a motion
bearing down on you – an accumulation
of stars, each night of them
arranging over the roofs of entire cities.

His careful strokes whiten the web,
the swirl of woodgrain blotted
like a breath stopped
at the heart. Nothing has changed
you say, faithlessly. But something has
cleansed you past recognition. When
you stand near his ladder looking up
he does not acknowledge you,
and as from daylight in a dream you see
your house has passed from you
into the blessed hands of others.

This is ownership, you think, arriving
in the heady afterlife of paint smell.
A deep opening goes on in you.
Some paint has dropped onto your shoulder
as though light concealed an unsuspected
weight. You think it has fallen through
you. You think you have agreed to this,
what has been done with your life, willingly.

Each Bird Walking

Not while, but long after he had told me,
I thought of him, washing his mother, his
bending over the bed and taking back
the covers. There was a basin of water
and he dipped a washrag in and
out of the basin, the rag
dripping a little onto the sheet as he
turned from the bedside to the nightstand
and back, there being no place

on her body he shouldn't touch because
he had to and she helped him, moving
the little she could, lifting so he could
wipe under her arms, a dipping motion
in the hollow. Then working up from
the feet, around the ankles, over the
knees. And this last, opening
her thighs and running the rag firmly
and with the cleaning thought
up through her crotch, between the lips,
over the V of thin hairs —

as though he were a mother
who had the excuse of cleaning to touch
with love and indifference
the secret parts of her child, to graze
the sleepy sexlessness in its waiting
to find out what to do for the sake
of the body, for the sake of what only
the body can do for itself.

So his hand, softly at the place
of his birth-light. And she, eyes deepened
and closed in the dim room.
And because he told me her death as
important to his being with her,
I could love him another way. Not
of the body alone, or of its making,
but carried in the white spires of trembling
until what spirit, what breath we were
was shaken from us. Small then,
the word *holy*.

He turned her on her stomach
and washed the blades of her shoulders, the
small of her back. 'That's good,' she said,
'that's enough.'

On our lips that morning, the tart juice
of the mothers, so strong in remembrance, no
asking, no giving, and what you said, this
being the end of our loving, so as not to hurt
the closer one to you, made me look
to see what was left of us
with our sex taken away. 'Tell me,' I said,
'something I can't forget.' Then the story of
your mother, and when you finished
I said, 'That's good, that's enough.'

FROM AMPLITUDE

(1987)

What sort of times are these?
And who has a clear conscience?

Eat, drink and be thankful! –
But how can I do this
If my food belongs
To the starving
My drink to the parched?

At the same time, I eat and drink.

DEREK MAHON,
'Brecht in Svendborg'

If Poetry Were Not a Morality

It is likely I would not have devoted myself to poetry in this world
which remains insensitive to it, if poetry were not a morality.
        JEAN COCTEAU,
        Past Tense

I'm the kind of woman who
when she hears Bobby McFerrin sing without words
for the first time on the car radio has to
pull over and park with the motor
running. And Cecil Taylor, I pulled over
for him too, even though later the guy
at the record store said he was just
a 'side man'. Something he did with silence and
mixing classical with I'm-worried-about-this-but-I-
have-to-go-this-way-anyhow. *This* not letting me
go. What did you do, the guy asked me, when you
pulled over? Smiled, I said, sat

and smiled. If the heart could be that simple. The photo
of Gandhi's last effects taped near
my typewriter: eyeglasses, sandals, writing paper
and pen, low lap-sized writing desk and something
white in the foreground like a bedroll.
Every so often I glance at this, just paper torn
from a book, and wish I could get down to
that, a few essentials, no
more. So when I left this place it would be
humbly, as in those welfare funerals my mother
used to scorn because the county always bought

the cheapest coffins, no satin lining, and if you
wanted the dead to look comfortable
you had to supply your own
pillow. I still admire her hating to see the living
come off cheap in their homage to any life. She
was Indian enough so the kids used to
taunt me home with 'Your mother's a squaw!'
Cherokee, she said. And though nobody
told me, I knew her grandfather had to be
one of those chiefs who could never

get enough horses. Who, if he had two hundred,
wanted a hundred more and a hundred more
after that. Maybe he'd get up in the night and go
out among them, or watch their grazing

from a distance under moonlight. He'd pass his mind
over them where they pushed their muzzles into
each other's flanks and necks and their horseness
gleamed back at him like soundless music until
he knew something he couldn't know
as only himself, something not to be told again
even by writing down the doing

of it. I meet him like that sometimes,
wordless and perfect, with more horses than he
can ride or trade or even know why
he has. His completeness needs to be stern, measuring
what he stands to lose. His eyes
are bronze, his heart is bronze with the mystery
of it. Yet it will change his sleep
to have gazed beyond memory, I think, without sadness or
fear onto the flowing backs of horses. I look down
and see that his feet are bare, and I
have never seen such beautiful prideless feet set
on the earth. He must know what he's doing, I think, he
must not need to forgive himself the way I do

because this bounty pours onto me
so I'm crushed by surrender, heaped and
scattered and pounded into the dust with wanting more,
wanting feet like that to drive back
the shame that wants to know why
I have to go through the world like an overwrought
magnet, like the greedy braille of so many
about-to-be-lost memories. Why I can't just
settle down by the side of the road and turn the music
up on one of those raw uncoffined voices of
the dead – Bob Marley, Billie Holiday or the way Piaf
sang 'Je Ne Regrette Rien' – so that when

the purled horse in the music asks what I want with it
we are swept aside by there being no answer except
not to be dead to each other, except for
those few moments to belong beyond deserving to
that sumptuousness of presence, so the heart
stays simple like the morality of
a robin, the weight of living so clear a mandate
it includes everything about this junkshop
of a life. And even some of our soon-to-be deadness
catches up to us
as joy, as more horses than we need.

His Shining Helmet; Its Horsehair Crest

I was reading the novel
about a war fought on horseback, reading
with the pleasure of a child given horror as
splendor. The moment came when
the soldier rose in his saddle and
the rim of the saddle was shorn
away. There the story broke off.
Then the survey of fallen comrades and
the field trampled around those with
'wounds to the head and breast'. Strange
how I thought of the horses during
these tinted portraits, the horses, mentioned
only as 'he rode', 'his mount
stumbled', or 'he bent from
the saddle to retrieve the standard, then
galloped on'.

I close the book and see then
the one they did not speak of – the one
wounded in the face, the one
with his hand caught in the mane of
his horse, which lies beside and
over him, its eyes still open and its breath
a soft plunging to which the novelist
would add a 'light rain' or
'a distant thunder of cannons'.

But in the closed book, this
is the long moment I look into – the future
in which the wounds, as they say in the manual,
will be 'non-specific, though
fatal'. How far
from the single admonition in the Hittite cavalry
instructions, simply to: 'Kill
the horse.'

Refusing Silence

Heartbeat trembling
your kingdom
of leaves
near the ceremony
of water, I never
insisted on you. I admit
I delayed. I was the Empress
of Delay. But it can't be
put off now. On the sacred branch
of my only voice – I insist.
Insist for us all,
which is the job
of the voice, and especially
of the poet. Else
what am I for, what use
am I if I don't
insist?
There are messages to send.
Gatherings and songs.
Because we need
to insist. Else what are we
for? What use
are we?

That Kind of Thing

I'm ready to climb into the shower
at the luxury hotel in Bahia when he
arrives, the Information Officer
from the American Consulate of Salvador.
I'd just said to Ray, 'I feel like we've
walked straight into a bank
where they keep people' – and this suite
invented, like the word 'posh', by somebody
serious about pleasure in an off-handed
way. And this man – off-
handed too in a khaki shirt so tight on him

the buttons ripple open when he
sits down, revealing little jets of
flesh and chest hair.

So, crossing and uncrossing his
legs, he tells us what to expect: don't
wear jewelry into town or, if we do,
to make sure any chains we wore
were really gold, so when the thieves
yanked them from our necks we
wouldn't be beheaded. A woman had
walked into his office just the other day
with her throat ripped – one of those cheap
metal neck-chains – though he didn't want
to alarm us. And the tourist who met
a man with a pistol outside his hotel who
said to give him his wedding ring and when it
wouldn't come off, the bandit
put the man's finger into his mouth and
sucked on it and said: this ring
is going to come off or I'll bite it
off. Ray lights up a cigarette, maybe even
two cigarettes, and slides the glass
balcony door open so the smoke can go out.
The ocean-sound comes in like an invisible
waterfall standing somewhere in the room
where we sit, eighteen floors up and,
as the receptionist said – not to worry,
'every room with a water view'.

'You're just in time to see the sunset,'
says the Information Officer of
Salvador. 'But did
the ring come off?' I ask.
'Oh sure,' he says, with an air of the less
than trivial, this matter of rings
and fingers. 'A lot of poverty here. A lot of
hunger.' He's got a year to go in Salvador,
one of those places, he wants us to know, not
on the top of anyone's assignment list, even
a man like him, who's served most of
his time in Third World Countries – the gist
of his feeling being: they don't call them
'under-developed' for nothing.

Discussing then, the plight of
university professors working for so little
they have to hold sometimes three, four jobs –
the Information Officer somehow relating this
to his important friend who
ran a golf course, a food processing plant, and
a restaurant in another town – just to
make ends meet, we supposed, but never made
the connection. 'But the students, do they
support the professors in the strike?'
'Oh, sure, students will go with anything
that's against the government. The reactionary
left. They'd like to make a revolution, but
just when they're supposed to
demonstrate – it rains and they cancel
out – or the sun shines and it's such a nice
day they have to go to
the beach. No, it's a hard place
to be a revolutionary,' he says, as if he'd
been one himself in some former
incarnation. But he's gone on to more dignified
pursuits as befits a man who represents
a government whose banks have bankrolled debts
so colossal its bankers would have to
confiscate whole countries
to turn this thing around, a man with
diapers to change – with a savvy glance in my
direction, protecting his flank, having dropped
news of his Japanese wife who 'poops out'
around 6 p.m. every night. 'That woman
loves to cook!' and only the night before
'knocked out a banquet (does all the cooking
herself). May is our busy month.' They
haven't seen much of Brazil but got
down to São Paulo where the wife
spotted some hamburger joints and they hit
McDonalds, a Big Boy and a Whopper – one, two,
three – that woman who loves
to cook. Jumping then

to this baby whose diaper might at this very
moment need changing, so he had to
get back, but whatever we needed, not
to hesitate. Give him a call. 'That's what

126

I'm here for,' (in this hell hole, he
seemed to want to add). Then as
afterthought, we'd need an interpreter –
'It's a problem. I have to do everything
in Portuguese,' he says, as if apologizing for
some deaf mute we'd eventually have to
meet. His hand out to me, but

speaking to Ray: 'I read your stuff. Well
written. But, to be perfectly
honest, too depressing. I have to live
with that kind of thing
down here all the time.' His hand cast
over his shoulder at the city. 'Know
what I mean? But well written.' Pumping
my hand then and us
not supposed to hesitate, but the waterfall
drowning out whatever else as the door

closed and we sat back on the couch,
smiling crazily
under the palm fronds
in the smoke-filled vault
with the lights of Salvador
shining in the distance and the Information
Officer of Salvador
gone home to his duties.

[Bahia, Brazil, 1984]

In Maceio

She gave me the flowers —
two armfuls of red iris backed with
fern fronds and this red, red of
parrot feathers, red
of a death shout, of any heart's
last breath. As we started to move
from the lecture room to leave them
behind, she gave me the flowers.
I said what are they called in
Portuguese? She
smiled, shook her head and no one else
knew either. But she wanted
me to know, she was giving me
the flowers. Not just
decoration on the table behind which
I stood to tell the night students
about poetry in America. They
were dying, these flowers, in the heat of
my English flowing over the tired students.
'But they're stupid, these students,'
Eduardo said. Eduardo who spent his nights
with them and had to
do it, though he meant to love them and
did, working two jobs himself — a professor
on strike at the University, needing more
pay, making it up with these
night students, 'these ones' who, he said, wanted
more and who came stupid and mostly stayed
stupid while they got an education.
But she gave me the flowers, picked them up
in her two arms as we started to leave them
behind to be thrown out with
the trash. She gave me
the flowers and I said did you
understand what I said? and she said 'Yes',
maybe the only English she knew and she
put the red flowers with no name
into my arms, and we walked out of there.

Sugar

The restaurant's expensive and German, but
it's Porto Alegre and the American to
my left has just delivered us
like so much pulpy meat
the six hours from Florianopolis, him
driving, he thinks, like a real
Brazilian. But without their confidence in
Death as the one reliable card
in the deck waiting to turn up no matter how
careful you are. So what the hell! Why not
live in the rush of cosmic benevolence tested
by the far side of what limits kill
of desire – instead of letting chance get
flabby, letting your hand
cool on the throttle like a mortician's palm

on your kneecap? But no, this well-meaning
fellow put fear in the car like a huge,
noxious bouquet of forget-me-nots, put
betrayal, put loss in the shape of
his young wife who'd left that very morning
and taken their child with her back to
America and the good life. He flung him-
self at Death like confetti. And I swear
I saw Death dust off his proud shoulders,
shake his black mane, throw back his
huge head and laugh that beautiful
wreck of a laugh that knows
exactly where it's going. Death

doesn't want the bride-
groom. I had opportunity to see that,
between one near-miss and the next
expertly negotiated curve. No, Death is like
a busy man with something else
on his mind while he does
what he's going to
do. The way he took my friend's
husband who'd gone to the garden to dig a few
potatoes for supper. She heard his spade
strike the concrete walkway and saw
through the kitchen window his face pushed
into the soft, dark furrow. So I kept
the conversation lively

all the way, while my dear-
est and only slept off terror in the back seat.
Then we arrived at this marvelous feast.
The American to my left, as if
confirming poison in the glass I'd just taken
a drink from, leaned over and said, 'Look around
you. You don't see any brown faces here, do
you?' In Rio the brown-faced novelist from
Buenos Aires who said, 'They either killed or
deported them. Yes, the faces get whiter
the farther south you go.' And yes, the faces

at our table are white, so white
Nora's story about the last time she took sugar
in her coffee stays with me
like a requiem. 'We went back to the town
where my mother was raised,' she said, watching
the others ladle sugar
into their strong, black coffee. 'And there
on the street, we saw
the man who'd been engaged to my mother
at the time my father stole her
away. He was a doctor and everyone in
the family thought he would have made a better
husband than my father. Who knows? Maybe
they were right. We saw him crossing
the street. My father grabbed hold
of my mother like he was afraid she might run
back to him, and said, "There's that man! Let's

get out of here." That night when the waiter
offered sugar, my father said, as he always said,
"No sugar." I must have been feeling some
solidarity with my father because when the waiter
came to me, I also said, "No sugar." I was
thirteen years at the time and it
was the 6th of February, 1947. From that day on
I have never taken sugar in
my coffee – a real Oedipus
complex.' Then someone in the company corrected
her and said, 'No, a real *Electra*
complex.' And everyone agreed and said the word
Electra, either outloud or
to themselves, *Electra*, as they tasted for a
moment, the sugar – the sweet black
sugar in those thick cups of coffee we were about
to drink together.

130

If Blood Were Not as Powerful as It Is

From the open market with its tangy smell
of salted meats and caged birds into
this coolness – the Golden Chapel
of Recife where Christ too is gold-
encrusted and the rays spiking
from his golden head
set off the irregular rays of blood
streaming down his forehead, blood which
would be golden too, if blood
were not as powerful as it is – powerful
enough to avoid even gold.

We sign the guest book and stand
before the glass showcase
where another Christ, lit up like
an expensive jewel, reclines
with his knees slightly
bent. A rivulet trickles from his rib cage
and stops without dropping
one precious drop – this heavenly body
that bleeds without bleeding.

In a dark alcove, a third Christ
is displayed on his back.
I can't see his face. Monks beckon
to either side and I see he is dressed
as they are, in the brown robe
of the Third Order of St Francis.
The soles of his long, thin feet, each
with the blood-sign where the missing nails
joined him to the cross, are tilted
into view where he lies on the wooden cart.

Then I notice Mary – the black arches
of her eyebrows lifted so they mean she
will plead for eternity and not be
answered as she gazes upon these replicas
of what was her son – his own eyes
peacefully closed in a beauteous pain
that flows outward the more he tries
to hold it in. And she,
the woman in the doorway as we start to leave,

has asked for and is given
a glass into which the attendant is pouring
water from a bottle kept
for that purpose. Someone
hovers behind her and she brushes them away
as she drinks, so as to drink
deeply enough to get past the fear of the next
thirsting. She drinks
and lifts her eyes, drinks and
watches, then calls

to the other and offers up the glass to be
filled again, which the attendant does,
obedient, for now, to what our guide calls
'the informal sector'. Then I remember
at the Consulate, talk of drought
five years running in regions
to the South, how these people have come
into the cities for food, for
water. The face
behind her shoulder looks up: Mary
of Recife, who needs water, who
lets him give her
the water
she has been waiting for.

[Recife, Brazil, June 1984]

Redwing

The readers of poetry, the writers of
poetry. Nation inside
the nation. That rainbow holding briefly over
the Strait of Juan de Fuca, its violet
inner rim, its guess-work dome
of crimson. My back to the sun for this
to happen at all, the eye extending
its shadow until it sees into
what it doesn't see. I don't have to think
of raindrops hanging as light, or to command

132

the schoolbook corpses of refraction and
internal reflection to be dazzled. The myth
of the Vilela Indians, its rainbow
a gigantic serpent charmed
by a small girl until it sheds her
sway and piecemeal ravages the world, vanquished
at last by an army of birds – that's good enough
for me. And victory too, each bird
dipping itself in the blood
of the monster.

With Stars

My mother speaks from the dark – why
haven't I closed my eyes? Why don't I
sleep? And when I say I can't, she
wraps the quilt around me and leads me
to the window. I am four years old and
a star has the power of wishes.
We stare out together, but she sees past
their fierce shimmering sameness, each
point of light the emblem
of some lost, remembered face. What
do they want? I ask. 'Not to be
forgotten,' she says, and draws me close.
Then her gaze sifts the scattered brilliance.
Her hand goes out – 'There! that one!' so
her own mother, dead years back, looks down
on us. Sleep then like a hammer
among the orbiting dead.

Tonight it is the stars reminding
keeps me up past midnight.
My mother's voice, as in that childhood room,
is with me so surely I might rush out
and find that window, those stars
no further than the next doorway, and her
there waiting – awake all night
because I was awake. 'Go
to sleep,' I'd say. 'They want me

awake tonight.' And she'd know who I meant –
those others still living and afar
because I think them there. And why not
give the dead this benefit of separations?
There were so many nameless before.
But oh, if one falls, *if* –
how can that child ever fall asleep
until sunrise?

Dim House, Bright Face

(for my brother, Denzel)

She still cries over that dead child,
and for years would bring him up
with strangers who came to the house.
Unashamed to weep freshly, she took again
the cheaply framed school photograph
and passed it from hand to
hand. The boy's open gaze into that forward time,
laden then with calamity
because it seemed, to the minds of those unwary
visitors, that he knew his silence
had another meaning, one that entered
theirs and caused those moments to almost
make a sound they each
withheld.

So she softened his ongoing future in her heart
with their unreceivable comfort. Took
back the photograph and put it
in the drawer, as if to shield him
from their inrushing eagerness
to hear of those other faces on the mantle,
the ones who can't know yet what living
was.

The Borrowed Ones

(for Kate and Tessa)

We, the old children, are now old again
with a new authority. We take
their young hands in ours
and tell them we will stay old, swear
to grow even older, be rust
to their iron. Whose are these
rain barrels in the pasture that fill and over-
fill with softest rain? I knock them aside
and the ground drinks, in its gradual way,
all they give.

We were the motherless, or those who say 'Mother'
as 'help me', and whatever comes – that sky
with one orange bird, even a wave
that endures moonlight – even these
will do. Finally we did
for ourselves. In our loving we mothered
the men we wanted to be more than. And
though our breasts were still the breasts of
children, we gave ourselves as children
give, with the door wide open, with
the house on fire. Still, our hands were
mothers' hands, were lament and pledge,
a whirl of bells through the sweet gloom of
their foraging, and, yes, something, something was
satisfied.

If at our table those who would have loved us
ate the meal, forgetting to light
the candles, we smiled on them
with the kindness of conquered stars – not
the brightest ones, but those
expendable ones
that fall to gain a share
in the splendor.

Now, if I call you 'Daughter', it is not
out of obedience
you will step toward me
but as the ghost of one who bore you,
gazing out – I, who have given you
a daughter's arms.

All Day the Light Is Clear

Today I wished without mercy
in the bloodless nations of the mind
that a city had gone down with you
as in a war fought – not
on foreign soil, but here
in the part of the country I can't
do without. Then, if I wept for you
inexplicably, as I have
on street corners, I could say the name
of that city and ignite in the memories
of strangers, a companion
sorrow. 'Yes,' they would say, 'Yes,
we know,' giving again that name
like a fountain
in some dusty village where the women pause,
dash water across their brows,
and pass on.

And though I shame such power and force it
from my mind, you enter this street
as a touch on the shoulder, a stare that
speaks, or in the brief nods
between workers at change of shift.
I lean on their conquering faces.
I add you to the heap, to the beautiful
multitude for whom only singing
and silence may serve – those
of our city, city of the unmiraculous,
undiminished belonging, toward which
in the green fields – as did the women
of Leningrad – I bow, bow again
and make no sound.

Their Heads Bent
Toward Each Other Like Flowers

Those who hold themselves above suicide,
(and who could blame them?) would
make a joke of your efforts and how we both
survived. Sometimes I can't help myself and
a shred of the story slips out of the silence –
how I came into that house we shared
near the wise, gray Atlantic and, as one bewildered,
you showed me where the pistol went off suddenly,
unexpectedly, before you could lift it
to your head. 'There,' you said, and we looked up
to the neat bird-sized entry
in the plaster, stood like two guilty children
who've struck all the matches
in the empty house and singed
away their delicate eyebrows.

Again we stand – young husband, uncertain wife –
as I tell this to someone for whom it cannot matter,
though this too is necessary – to feel such minds
turn away, as mine did then
in worse than disbelief.
I was too safe in my young woman's body, too precious
as one is precious before the imagined death
one intends to accomplish later, much
later, and, if possible, only in poems
where the choosing is huge, is classic and belongs
to time, as we do not who serve no future. Or so
you tried, in your failed way, to tell me – I
who could not be loved, and so
seemed eternal.

Yours was that other bravery, the one worth mocking.
You lived on past your chosen death, and I,
who had a life, this ring of smoke
these fifteen years, at last emerge into another,
premature vacancy, bounded on all sides
with beginnings – this altered memory in which
the shot, as you intended, passes through us both,
and we are not here to end the story
with love and live on as we must.

Or perhaps love is only the apology
I invent to hold your place – until even that claim
is not needed, and you reappear
as one stronger even than memory, ungarlanded
by its sullen excess, its shadow-music
thrummed against the skull. At this threshold
you are willing even to do without
love – as I cannot – willing
at last to be forgotten.

Photograph of a Lighthouse Through Fog

I said: dark voyage, I am deeply wounded
      and desire still in me
            like an eel.
I said: shards and trembling.
Said: the golden light of the sea.
Said: I can not separate your light from
            your silence.

This reaches him like a photograph
of the lighthouse on a clear day. What is it
      for? this disabled
            windmill, this moon
     in armor?

     The rest without cunning or blame.
         Fog
rolls in with its 'vale of the soul', its
      fledgling obedience, daring to ask:
        where are we now?
      Caught in some ruby-throated
     pain; its staple of hope
         mercenary as the word
      eternity.

I said: vigil and a body that dies.
I said: heart not of this shore, the birds fly
      through me.

Said: I once lived dark
                    like honey, deepest in
                              pleasure after the pleasure.
Said: halo, memory dampens my
                    memory. I can't know
                              how far I shine.

Pain, he said, is advice I never take. Any cat
knows what to do in the aviary.

The photographer lashes the camera to his arm,
              hoping to record light as
                      inscription, its
                              baptismal slapping
              against the water.
              But is
    that salty staccato warning or invitation?

              Stay away, I said. *Stay*
                      away.

Small Garden Near a Field
(for Denzel)

While any two are talking, one,
without glimpsing it, has already shed
the confident smile of the living. You
were going first all our childhood. Youngest
of my brothers, I used you up, squandered
your fifteen years which can't remember itself
in its voiceless purpose. 'Twenty-three-years
today he's gone,' our mother said, as you ran
to the dresser to bring my hair brush. Twenty-
three-years as you put on your many coats, as you
bicycled through the neighborhood slinging newspapers
like fury onto porches in the crisp half-dawn.

How dead you wanted to be when you died! Each
stuttering moment pearled in the memory – how
I let you lean out of the dark into my car window
the night of your first prom. I can smell

the brash carnation in your buttonhole, imagine
the youngest kisses, those given innocently
before desire rakes like a searchlight across
the cool, the cruel valleys of love you
will never have. You click shut, kiss
shut, and won't live to April.

I roll down the window. You rest
your arms on my arm, grin shyness over
the chipped front tooth and don't want to say much
in front of her, the girl in taffeta and longing –
your first, last girl. Get in, I say, let's
cruise by where we don't live anymore. That house
a shack now, brambles and kids' toys, the willow
sagging into the street. It's right
to drive by, harm ourselves a little with
what comes after, push back
the goodness of the past so it doesn't cry out

unattainable. Goodness of
not enough beds so they sent you
into mine to be thralled sleepward with stories.
Language to you is still errand and magic
spiced with singing. I close my eyes
and remember yours open. I'm already a reader
of books, have begun to work that slow trench into
history. Babur – I tell you like treasure –
was the first Mughal Emperor of India, descended
from Genghis Khan and Timur
the Lame. Babur: Turkish for lion.

They have wrapped your head in gauze, my sultan,
the folds of your turban make a temple
where you lie. The conquering is over now
and we are laying out the garden you planned,
patterned after the remembered one
in Kabul. It won't be enough. 'In Agru,' you say,
'they have no horses, no grapes or muskmelon, no
ice or cold water, no baths or candles, no torches,
not a candlestick.' I snail your warmth
into mine, sleep night-long, death-long beside you,
legend to your unlived name which I carry
like a dead tree
with the live birds still in it.

Present

She could hold me with stories, even
those about people whose names and doings
were feathers, a fluttering at
the brain, scattered or wafted in the current
of her voice, softly away. Those lives
happened out of her and into me and out
again, because I couldn't remember, only be
warmed by them. Somehow my forgetting insured
returns to that hovering population in her
memory, of which, as I found, I was a part.

She said she thought maybe she couldn't have
children, maybe nothing would come. She
and my father together by then two years.
His being dead now, not coming into this, but
there too, as if he couldn't hear us,
but we could know for him. 'I'd go up into
the woods where he was logging, do what I could,
work hard as two men myself. That day

on Round Mountain your dad and his partner
got ahead of me. I'd been working.
I hadn't seen where I was. Suddenly I was
alone, walking this old logging road, fireweed
over my head. I stood still and listened
to the birds and other sounds – wind and
little fallings and shiftings in the undergrowth,
animal stirrings. It's so beautiful
here! I kept thinking. I've never been anywhere
so beautiful! I was alone with the mountain. Sun

shattering down through the trees onto ferns
and fallen logs. It's peaceful here, I thought.
Then it came to me, like the mountain had told
me, and I knew it was over. One waiting was
over. And another was starting. The feeling so
sure I put my hands on my belly and pressed
a little against where the carrying had started
before I'd known it. Knowing then, so you'd
stopped happening without me. 'We,' I thought,
'*We*.' And I thought of your father not

knowing yet, and it seemed you were knowing for
him already, were rushing ahead of me like
an action I had no part in, but was all of me
and some of him that I was about to let you tell
him. Isn't that what conception is? Agreeing
to take the consequences of things so far
beyond you that a trembling takes over and more
is shaken out of us than we can
possibly account for?' And something else, she
said, the elevation of mountains, the way

beauty makes things want to join
each other. Then far off, like an echo of
itself, the *swish-swish* of the crosscut,
the steady rhythm of the blade limber against
a tree. She started to walk, still thinking how
beautiful it was all around her, the partnership
of the saw blade raking through the silence
as she made her way toward the far away
splintering, the rending of the heartwood she
knew would fall, would crash down, shuddering

the length of itself against the trees still
standing, while like a deer, picking its way
through underbrush to the edge
of the clearing, she moved, until
they saw her back into human shape. A woman
whose whereabouts they had wondered vaguely
about as they worked. And as she joined them,
they kept on with their working.

Cougar Meat

Carried this morning in the dodge and swoop
of error, rethinking a breach
with a friend – how I'd failed to staunch harm
with kindness when she needed me
as sacrifice – then you, brother, came in
to say goodbye, hovered in my kitchen
for coffee. You'd been hunting cougar three days
and nights, with your dogs, somewhere

in the mountains back of Gardiner. You hadn't
slept, keeping the fever up until the magic
gave in to you. But on the third day
snow, the invisible current of pursuit
exchanged for tracks. The kill then, baffling
and simple – awesome death made perfunctory
with a shot. I hear you out, know why

you've come, certain of welcome, yet your act
hated for the usual 'female' reasons, or so
you think, and are freed of wonder and of
shame. Should I ask, Pharaoh, did you eat
of the heart? Did you find it sweet? Or,
in a bounty of silence, know the pelt
torn away, the carcass unquenchable where it fell
in its blue efficiency, its avalanche of
unmeaning which allows those man-sized footsteps
to point away unknown, yet deeply familiar. Mine
to ask whose wildness we are, whose trust
soon to be plundered? The adrenaline has let you
down. You're bone-weary and back with
the rest of us, diamond bright with hunger,

unfulfilled by the dominant courage here toward
livelihood with all its unedifying hazards.
Should I put aside kinship with the hunted and
the dumb, pray that cougars last for men like you?
Only in the mind's rarefied traffic with the sacred
have I met cougar. Could have gone all day, all
life not thinking *cougar*, had you kept
from here. Wild Horse Annie, in that same untutored
leap, defended mustangs in the Pryor Mountains,
never having laid eyes on one. Enough to guess
spirits of the West surviving in those rugged bands
pursued by helicopters. Her fear – the unseen loss,
more heritage in a Medicine Hat Pinto than
in the frontier mandate to take what

you can. 'Good eating too,' you say, still
talking cougar. 'The word is, it tastes like pork
or veal, not that I'd know.' You launch into story:
'That time Dad forgot his lunch and one of the guys
on the dock offered him a sandwich, which he
ate. At poker break, he said to the guy, "What
kind of sandwich was that, anyway?"
"Me-ow!" the guy said, and he didn't mean pussycat.

Dad looked at him, said "It's better than snake,
by God, better than flying squirrel, and I've
eat both with appetite to spare." Cougar meat!' my
brother says, like somebody has handed him a bat
on a skewer. *Not nature, but the visions she*

gave me, Rilke said. I kiss your cheek, brother,
where we stand on the porch. You're off
on your first vacation to an exotic place – Hawaii,
paradise regained, where you will lie down with
the lamb. You tell me you want your son brought up
to hunt cougar. If you die tomorrow in a plane crash,
I'm supposed to see to that. Don't
count on it, I say. Not one iota have I moved you,
but all day I wear dread in your name, and in the name
of Cougar, renewing in heart the biblical sacrifice of
Uzzah, whose unthinking touch on the Ark of the Covenant
was death to him, instruction for us. Recovering
that clear shot in the snow, these intricacies
of undoing, for which language was also given
to say: the meat was not wasted.

Message for the Sinecurist

The poet of nouns has left my attic.
Burn the wood, I said. Read
my books. Sleep under my roof, dream
and prosper. One thing in recompense
I asked. So was he late or
never, and made a landlord
of a friend. So was he my tenant
and missed the premise of those rooms
and rooftops.

When we had cleared away his locus
of debris, we sat and read his postcard
from the beauteous far place – clearly
his intentions so full of spine
and keen regret, but haste and sadness
had paraphrased him badly. We considered,
then put the card away.

144

I sit under the high pitch of rain again
and the birds thread through my days
with fresh regard. Yes, nouns, the nails,
the vigorous scaffold of each elected tree.
But then, my poet, the awful hammering
that knows as it does.

Simple Sonatina

Something is dying, but without blood or
writhing on any shore. Everything seems as
it was: no poets dignified with prison, none
banished or tortured. Each of us
has enough paper to write the histories of
several worlds. We don't fear the knock
at the door. And yet, this stench, this
oversweet stillness reaches even here
among the nations of spruce and hemlock,
head-high salal and the thorny devil's club.
That country I could speak with intimately
in myself, country Whitman honored, teeming
and lustrous, country I crossed and recrossed
like a thrown-out child until anywhere
wasn't home – something of that country

has made its dying spot in the woods,
and, slug-bellied with salvage, crawls away.
These are lying times, my friends, lying times.
Easy to say the varnished brutes want to cozy up
again, when *again* convicts. No heroics here.
I don't regret a single poem about 'the tawny-
throated nightingale', or simple duty
which 'hath no place for fear', or Longfellow's
'soft bells, and gleaming nights'. But something
of what I loved is alone in me now, as it is
for many who loved so. In this indifferent time
harmony wears too amiable a face, and I can't sing
'Melancholy Baby' any more.

The Story of a Citizen

Rain extravagantly that morning kept us
at the coffee shop, discussing what? Our era?
Not too grand to say – yes, and with the fervor
of young philosophy students. *Our* era which,
Alan said, would be known for its blatant political
pornography: 'No contours, only oscillating
transitions,' a phrase he applied like a seasoning
of butterflies to astound us past meaning. 'It
makes me want to puke,' Jerry said every so often.
'What does?' somebody finally asked. 'All of it,'
he said. Outside the rain coming down, insisting
on reverie, no one able to summarize the gut feeling
of having been stripped of the sacred on more than
one front, though it came down to that. Just
listening made you hunger for extremities,

anything to get beyond the synthetic equilibrium
of helplessness. Why not attempt the truly brazen?
Your friend's elevation of a dead dog into
negotiable value – this impressed you. You read
his novel twice, thinking he'd found the key
to selflessness. Yet dogs seemed so obvious, so
eminently popular. Kick one and a regiment of
defenders will taint your history. But,
like a government casting about for the right
passion to assist its military decor, a kick
was needed: so you kicked. Call it an evil instinct,
but there I was, as we scurried back to our jobs
in the downpour, a woman stopping to kick a dog that
had been tied to a parking meter, which already
insinuated that the dog wished to be elsewhere. My
kick had the authority of ownership, so no one passing

bothered to confuse it with cruelty, or fun.
The primitive takes over and raises such events beyond
interpretation into what might be called a 'detached
commission.' My kick was a serious kick, not based
on chance or deserving, but on the priorities of
ownership – which is an American pastime – to empty
that office of pleasure, to subdue it to the purely
civilian. I am thinking here of a ballet dancer who
praised the essentially military 'when put to civilian
uses,' who said: 'I enjoyed the Army very much indeed.

I was a courier. I was an interpreter... I had my own
jeep.' As the courier of my kick I acknowledged
the tyranny of being addressed as a civilian while
the oneiric appearance of weapons loomed symphonic
with extinction in the vestibule. This then becomes

the history of how I became a soldier – I,
whose only patriotic act had been the continued
love of myself in the body of a woman.
A woman forced through soldierly fear to
rejuvenate a childhood relationship with God.
A woman twice visited by ownership in marriage,
who invested tumultuously in the promise of love
eternal because it appealed to her among the other
friendly disengagements. That woman, that
self-appointed kicker of dogs, conscripted now
like every other woman, man and dog: woman who
waits uneasily for orders, who despises
her superiors, who once was a mist of tenderness,
who exudes savagery, who is apolitical which is
the tribe of the soldier, who sleeps like a corpse
at the feet of her master, who squirms

in the ranks, who thinks, 'A short nap
in the snow would be exceedingly nice,' whose
memory of a home-cooked meal has been obliterated
by the seepage of fear, whose hair was first cut
at the age of thirteen, whose flower is
the butterfly bush, who will die a civilian
among other civilian-cum-soldiers, whose enemy
is an evil instinct with an expanding agenda,
whose campaign is the Campaign Under Moonlight
which requires that she bay like a wolf
speaking through moonlight which is the hotline
to the spirits of her ancestors, telling them
of their civilian descendants, of dogs
and the masters of dogs, through which she was

domesticated, this wolf, who honors itself
as a woman, who carries the dead
in her body, whose name is Spako, meaning
'Bitch', for she does as she pleases, whose
curses have the power to come true, who can see
ghosts, whose star is the brightest, is
the Eye of the Dog, whose threshold is guarded
by the poets because they know the sacredness

of doorways, of ancient cornerstones under which
are the sacrificed, the bodies of the saints,
the civilian saints, to whom I swear allegiance,
though saint is a word in poverty
when the memories of nations die with them,
as our time would require of us: as the folk dance
begins, as we scorn such death.

Survival of a Heart

So few particles of bodyhood engine
their way past oblivion, that when it keeps
being the heart that's saved I have to
listen, consort with mine in its pleasant lair,
assume its rustling more dearly. Though why not
cherish the bladder or the nose, those in and
outs immune to honeycombs of soul
devices? Why not one poet to exalt 'Oh melancholy
elbow, oh chin, oh sweet pituitary, oh matchless
epiglottis!' To have been erotogenically sealed
by flat earth poesy makes me haunt
in my prime. Give me the mound and scoop
of fortune, Keats lingering on 'a naked waist', or
Dickinson with moss on her lips, before I
dive this interior earthward. If after all
the Egyptians prevail and heart is
the requisite miser fit only to fling back at
gods who fondle and foul us, you, little dancer,
must tell it all – what scrapes and scraps and
summer lightning we had in the body's
swallow. Meanwhile, think on Voltaire's demise:
last minute maneuvers with the clergy to avert
the lime pit, then parcelled out, his brain to
the apothecary, his heart secured by
the Marquis de Villette, his body
driven off in one coach, his heart in
another, the coffin retrieved after thirteen years
from Scellières, 'brought in triumph' to Paris,
installed in the Panthéon, the coffin opened
finally to pay homage but found empty having been
pillaged by fanatics, its contents thrown
onto the rubbish heap. The jar wherein sloshed
his brain sold at auction to an unknown
buyer, the heart – that long suffering scoffer –
bequeathed to the Bishop of Orléans who put it
on the block. Napoleon III 'acquired' it, gave it
to the National Library in Paris where, as
the biographer said, it sits 'next to the products
of his brain'. Now, little coach, go your way.

Into the Known

(for Bill Knott)

A corpse has walked across my shadow.
How do I know? I was standing
so it fell darkly across the shadow of a tree
in water, and my shadow grabbed hold
in the branches and shouted, 'I'm drowning!
Save me!' Okay, I said, and stepped
to the side a few paces, disengaging its
arms from the leaves rippling through
me. But two boys rowed over it, dipping
their oars through my breasts and
groin. 'Save yourself!' my shadow cried.
But when I walked jauntily upstream, it
scraped along behind as usual, sure of
itself as a corpse is sure, so it speaks
to no one, yet holds our attention resentfully
like a cow in the roadway.

A gull rowed over me and I felt
feverish, as if my future meant to initiate
a moment I would soon have to avoid.
Time to rehabilitate your astonishment, I said
to myself and plunged on
into the known. A carriage
with two cream-colored horses pulls up, as I
knew it would, and my shadow gets out. She
comes up to me like she means to slap me,
but I turn my back quick! so she falls
over the necks of the horses and they tremble
and jangle their bits and lift their hooves
smartly in place on the pavement.

Yes, today a corpse put its inaugural hand
on my shoulder, on my shadow's silken
shoulder, like a sword through meringue.
Veil of white, veil of drowned breath – I was
sticky with it, plundered like a wren's nest.
Down I lay in the grass and down
like a dog to roll, but my shadow jumped
into me – retouching the real with
the real, as the mortician said.
Pianissimo, dread fumbled the length of me,
a safari of butterflies skimming the lunge
of a gravesite. I kept breathing

as long as I could, convulsively snatching
the breaths back into me, but my mind
kept seeing a sailboat with its sail
gone slack. And because I know something about
wind, how it fidgets and stampedes, then
forgets entirely so everything goes still,
I folded my hands on my breasts
and let things take their course, and let
the sun shine deeply upon me, and let
the carriage sulk near the walnut grove,
and the cream-colored horses neigh to other
horses and, in starlight, cloud-shadows
drowsy as a mind that can't shout, can't
beseech – let these drift over the beloved
corpse of my shadow. Suddenly then

I pull myself up! 'Not me!' I say.
I make them dance – that mitten, my shadow –
that quisling, my corpse. I dance
like a woman led to a vault of spiders.
I tell the horses to
dance too. I still don't know
if we got out of it.

The Hands of the Blindman

(for Jerry Carriveau)

In the square room
without windows
where the hours fill our pockets
with soft money, you reach
for simple things: the circle
of ash, the cup, its warm
liquid eye, the telephone, its knowing
that voices are always blind.

Walking from work, you wave fire
past your cigarette. There
is the hand of the stranger, now
the muzzles of dogs, the
rain. Touching my face once, you
were the rain, the stranger –
yet never did anyone in the dark
leave hands on me as you.

Rijl

To be a child named after a star
is to be given earth and heaven too, never
to find the dark unpossessive where you stand,
enraptured to the ground. Foot
of the Giant, Rijl al Musalsalah – Foot of the Woman
in Arabic, Heaven's Great General to
the Chinese who invented lotus feet for their women –
not just the foot miniaturized, but folded so
the underside of heel and
toes press together to blunt each step with
helplessness. Such a walker

I saw once near the Forbidden Palace
in Beijing, accompanied by her granddaughter.
Their hobbled steps still fresh to the mind that knows
there were poets who praised this exchange of pain

for beauty. I stumble among these duller earth-stars
to hang giants of another kind, so that from your sky
overflowing with immortals, you will look down
as we look up, to feel distance as kinship, splendor
as the white heads of our mothers. Algebar,
who must step as the giant bids, even

into the sea, though empowered
to survive there. Read in the legend
his interlude of blindness, how he wept on the shore –
Orion-the-hunter, the cannibal god-giant of Egypt
inscribed on the tombs as Sahu, a man running
with his head turned over his shoulder, 'fleet
of foot, wide of step'. And what is blindness but
the head upended in the foot so the body is all temple
or none? Intention, that willful god
of the strong, can't send a swallow from clocktower to

clothesline, yet you, child, sweep up the room, and
dancing with your arms over your head, command
to be joined, for yours is a double star, white-hot
and tinged with blue. I am your giant,
delivered to sight, going heart-in-heart
where you lead. Rai al Jauzah, herdsman of the stars,
it is winter where I write, and you are gleaming
above the hemlock, talisman
of a guardian joy. Not to you, but to the real girl
I turn, recalling a night when, dashing
from the house, she refused her sweater, calling back
for us all, 'Don't you know I'm
a star? Don't you know
                    I'm burning up?'

Bonfire

(for Ray)

The inflections of joy. The inflections of
                  suffering. And strangely
      sometimes the mixing
            of the two.
It reminds me of opening the huge *International*
      Butterfly Book with over 2000 species
          illustrated in color
     and among them, the giant birdwing butterfly
         Ornithoptera victoriae
obtained when John McGillivray, aboard the HMS
            Rattlesnake
      used a shotgun to bring it down
           somewhere in the Pacific.
Other wild petals shattered by use of
         pronged arrows
              in New Guinea.
And the laughable 'mechanical butterfly' intended
      as a decoy, said to be 'very successful' in
         capturing the flashing
            blue Morpho.

So many kinds of crying. So much raw gaiety,
      variegated with glittering
           silence. And you,
      my sudden bouquet,
who came to me awkwardly at the head of the stairwell
        outside the room that sheltered
          for so many nights
     our sleeping and loving.
            To weep there
                together
with death all handsomely in view,
         all open before us
     as the sea at night.
         All tenderly
     wild in that calm.

Safe midnight, your arms strong to hold my face into
            yours
      while the miracle of living raked
    its silky rapier down our backs.

The last time I kissed a man in fear
                    my first love went to war.
But I kissed you anyway – that seal of life, letter
                    sent and received
                                    in an instant.

Once in Quebec I drank cognac in the snow and
                                    on a dare
                    ice skated with my
                            friend's violin.
I'd been falling all day, diving into flesh
                            like a spirit half
                    in, half out
                                of the world.
But give me a perishable, fragile beauty
            that belongs to someone else and I skate
                    like music, like
                        the wizard of
                            the hopeful.
How many times I saved myself on behalf of
            that borrowed, that shuddering
                            violin!
When I handed it back he played his bonfire
                    of thanksgiving. Played
            a mazurka, then a jig, then
                        something vast
                    and aching
as when love must go on and at the same time
                                    perish.

I'm talking about memory now, that moment
            in which the doctor's news
                    flushed us through with dread,
                            and I hadn't swerved
                    back yet
into life. Even then I didn't forget you, violin
        who threw yourself into my arms,
                    violin asking not to
be broken one more time.
            It wasn't for music
                    you came to me, but
                            for daring ⇁ mine
                    and yours.
When they have to, they will write in the Book
        of Welcome:

                    Two darlings, two darlings.

Amplitude

Twice this Christmas Day you tried
to get somebody to listen with
you to the new Ricky Scaggs tape somebody
gave you, and were
refused. You bummed cigarettes, ate
some hot pickles, ranged in and
out of the house, played a game of
'Fish' with your kids, dangling
a magnet from a string
over eight little magnet-mouthed
fish that snapped open their yaps, then
clamped shut before your mag-
net could suck onto them and lift
them out of the wind-up pond
on the coffee table. Your kids beat
you and laughed about
it. You laughed
too, a little. Then clearly
had to find something else
to do. Dinner settled in on our mother, her
mouth open to that other magnet, sleep,
drawing her god knows where
out of our warm, swirling pond of family and
the still excited clutter of gift-
giving. Then you remembered Ray's Mercedes

parked near the swing set and said to me, 'Let's
go, Sis,' handing me the Scaggs tape. Imposs-
ible, though, to get out of
the house without your wife, Jean, and the
kids who wanted not
to miss out. Errands thought of too, so
it wouldn't be *just*
a ride, presents could be dropped
off to friends so there'd be some place to go
to. All of this okay. And the company
of your kids and wife adding
to the solitude
because of how they travel like a wake
behind you even when you're alone and
silent at your work. So the car

gliding effortlessly through the nearly
vacant streets, under the sparse dec-
orations of this mill town where we
were born, were kids together. Now, buckled in
to the dark, we adjust the volume and let
the cowboy sing his way down mainstreet, a
place he'll never see, with strangers he could care
less about. 'Will you shut up so I can hear
the song, for Chrissake,' you say into the back
seat, and, for a while we are all
with you, listening, because you said to, me
waiting until enough listening has gone by
to chance singing along, as you know
I have to, but not minding because it
beefs up the harmonies, a live track angling
in on studio vigor with the discrepancies
of the human. Real enjoyment leading then to

past hardship, so memory, that other fresh-
ness, cuts in to add value in a parallel key: 'Did
you ever think, when we were kids and bare-
foot in the logging camps, we'd drive up Race
Street in a Mercedes listening to cowboy
music?' We blotted out a bar
or two of aggressive banjo just marveling
at the unlikelihood. Vaguely, the
sense we shouldn't take such uncomplicated pleasure in
for long, or a magnet might
drop straight through the
roof and snatch one of us a-
way. Then, one by one,
the rest. But delight, pure
and simple, thanks to Ray's Mercedes, for having
pulled a fast one on this town and the in-
visible net over all, that said: You
won't amount to
a damn. And the triumph of it not even ours

as we passed the cemetery, lightly
dusted with snow, and our father there
with the others who came to this place and called
it good enough to hold a life and let it
go – some even, like him, who intended
to die here. The importance
of that choice unmade for me and humming along
with us. Then, looking over at you still

listening to the music, not
singing, but thinking about death or
whether or not you should be ashamed to be
seen motoring through the streets of our
hometown in the guise of those we'd learned to
hate as having more than their share. What

happened to those rocks we rushed from the house
to fling at bumper-to-bumper Californians, dragging
their mobile homes and over-
sized boats past the shack we were raised
in? In what far country did they
land, those heart-flung shards
of our untutored contempt? Here. They
landed here. And pelt down
because the violence of a kid's arm
is attached to more than stones and what
the world thinks of anyone's chances. Who's
to say if we could swing down Caroline Street and
pick up those two vigilantes they wouldn't
climb in – glad to have such mild
benefactors – ride along in wordless
awe, then the minute we put them out, set to
with a slingshot? Meanwhile I'm bartering
in the black markets of the mind for

the peace of a front yard nativity where
a kid's bike has tipped refreshingly onto the
baby Jesus so the spokes enhance his re-
solve toward bliss. Belief – the unspectacular
locomotion of childhood, gleams unremittingly
at me through the backlit curtains of
the house – that pyramid of wooly
lights anchored in the shadowy boughs. All
silent. All calm. House after
house. Until we hit
town and a little life stirs
outside the M & C tavern, two women
piloting a wobbly man into a back seat, then
genial shadows as they too climb in, reach
for the ignition and jerk away
from the curb. Suddenly over us a sign

above the used car lot: 'Save Ethiopia! Send
money now.' Our town shoots out into the starlit
map of the world where last night's TV news-
caster, in a voice dulled by the
ritualization of caring, hovers in-
visibly over a mother who has crawled forty miles
through desert with her child tied to
her back and will, he gives us
to understand, likely die
anyway. The bounce in the ad-break following
hurtles resourcefully on: 'In a moment, how *you*
can pick up the tab on African hunger.'
Ricky Scaggs careens into another verse
of relentless heartbreak, but it can't lift
an eyelid to this. Nor, inexplicably, that day

my high school chum, driving me down
Blue Mountain Road in his first car, hit
a child's puppy that had run in front of the
car, killing it outright. The kid weeping and
cuddling the mess and my friend, in a frenzy
of remorse, fumbling a dollar bill into
the kid's shirt pocket, then wordlessly sliding
into the seat beside me to drive us
away. That action waving like a white flag
of surrender over a trench whose once embattled
defenders are safely imprisoned
elsewhere. Passing now the pulp mill and

my brother reminding me how our father
worked there three times, and quit
three times. The windows are fogged
with dirt and ingots of unhealthy,
fluorescent unlight. 'Imagine
day after day working in there,' I say, thankful
to dispose of a safely impossible fate
so near at hand. My brother looks hard at
the place, then like he could bash it
to bits, his voice low and even: 'Jean's dad
spent thirty-nine years
in there.' She makes a sharp
noise in the dark to let her father out
again and into his well-earned death. We drive

onto the spit of land that lets us look back
across the harbor at the lights of
the town. More red
in their glimmer tonight, I think, and then,
more gold. 'It's
pretty,' Jean says, 'isn't
it?' The kids in their surplus of quiet, dreamily
then, 'Yes, pretty. Really
pretty.' We idle in the excellent rigor of
engine-pull de-
signed by Germans, until the same
child-voices, discarding beauty and
death as unequal to the moment, plead us
back 'in time,' as they put it, to give – unopened,
the gifts we are bearing.

MOON CROSSING BRIDGE

(1992)

For Ray

The world is gone,
I must carry you.

PAUL CELAN

from *Poems of Paul Celan*
translated by Michael Hamburger

I

Furious dreams, rivers of bitter certainty,
decisions harder than the dreams of a hammer
flowed into the lovers' double cup,

until those twins were lifted into balance
on the scale: the mind and love, like two wings.
— So this transparency was built.

PABLO NERUDA

100 Love Sonnets, LIV
translated by Stephen Tapscott

Yes

Now we are like that flat cone of sand
in the garden of the Silver Pavilion in Kyōto
designed to appear only in moonlight.

Do you want me to mourn?
Do you want me to wear black?

Or like moonlight on whitest sand
to use your dark, to gleam, to shimmer?

I gleam. I mourn.

Red Poppy

That linkage of warnings sent a tremor through June
as if to prepare October in the hardest apples.
One week in late July we held hands
through the bars of his hospital bed. Our sleep
made a canopy over us and it seemed I heard
its durable roaring in the companion sleep
of what must have been our Bedouin god, and now
when the poppy lets go I know it is to lay bare
his thickly seeded black coach
at the pinnacle of dying.

My shaggy ponies heard the shallow snapping of silk
but grazed on down the hillside, their prayer flags
tearing at the void – what we
stared into, its cool flux
of blue and white. How just shaking at flies
they sprinkled the air with the soft unconscious praise
of bells braided into their manes. My life

simplified to 'for him' and his thinned like an injection
wearing off so the real gave way to
the more-than-real, each moment's carmine
abundance, furl of reddest petals

lifted from the stalk and no hint of the black
hussar's hat at the center. By then his breathing stopped
so gradually I had to brush lips to know
an ending. Tasting then that plush of scarlet
which is the last of warmth, kissless kiss
he would have given. Mine to extend a lover's right past its radius,
to give and also most needfully, my gallant hussar,
to bend and take.

Wake

Three nights you lay in our house.
Three nights in the chill of the body.
Did I want to prove how surely
I'd been left behind? In the room's great dark
I climbed up beside you onto our high bed, bed
we'd loved in and slept in, married
and unmarried.

There was a halo of cold around you
as if the body's messages carry farther
in death, my own warmth taking on the silver-white
of a voice sent unbroken across snow just to hear
itself in its clarity of calling. We were dead
a little while together then, serene
and afloat on the strange broad canopy
of the abandoned world.

Corpse Cradle

Nothing hurts her like the extravagance
of questions, because to ask is
to come near, to be humbled at the clotted nucleus.
One persistent cry bruises her cheekbones and she lets
it, lets the open chapel of her childhood brighten over
her with tree-light. Gray-white future
of alder, hypnosis of cedar as when
too much scent-of-nectar combs
her breathing. Rain on rain
like an upsurge in his sudden need to graze her
memory, bareheaded at the quayside
where he dreamily smoked a cigarette and guided her,
the satin shell of her stillness, toward
that same whiteness at the top of rain, swollen
and gradual. How lucid she is,
blurred edgeless, like listening
to be more wide awake, that music she pressed into him
in order to fascinate what beautifully
he had begun. All bird and no recall, she
thinks, and lives in his birdness, no burden
but strange lightness so she wants to be up at dawn,
the mountains fogged with snow, a world
that sleeps as if it were
all the world and, being so, able to be seen
at its beginning, freshly
given as sleep is, bleak fertility of sleep when
she thinks far into his last resting
wherein she drifted, drifts, slow and white,
deeply asking, deep with its dark below.

Reading the Waterfall

Those pages he turned down in peaks
at the corners are kerchiefs now, tied
to the last light of each favorite tree
where he paused, marking my path
as surely as if he'd ordered squads
of birds to rustle leaves overhead.

And I do look up often, musing into
his warmed-over nests or letting
a thrum of recognition pulsate *koto*-like
as if his head were over my shoulder
in a cool fog allowed to think its way
down a marble staircase shorn
of its footfalls. In a child's crude
pea-pod canoe my amber beads float seaward
like a cargo meant to be lost.

How often I am held alive by half-a-matchstick,
remembering his voice across rooms
and going when called to hear some line
of poetry read aloud in our two-minded way
like adding a wing for ballast and
discovering flight.

So much of love is curved there
where his pen bracketed
the couplet mid-page, that my unused
trousseau seems to beckon deeply
like a forehead pressed into paradox
by too much invitation.

He lets me dress hurriedly for the journey
as a way to better leave me what vanishes
according to its readiness, as he is ready and glides now
into my long bedside Sunday
until we are like the dead pouring water
for the dead, unaware that our slender thirst
is unquenchable.

Trace, in Unison

Terrible, the rain. All night, rain
that I love. So the weight of his leg
falls again like a huge tender wing
across my hipbone. Its continuing – the rain,
as he does not. Except as that caress
most inhabited. Ellipsis of
eucalyptus. His arms, his beautiful
careless breathing. Inscription
contralto where his lips graze
the bow of my neck. Muslin half-light.
Musk of kerosene in the hall, fixative
to ceaselessly this rain, in which
there is nothing to do but be happy, be
free, as if someone sadly accused
came in with their coat soaked through
and said, 'But I only wanted
to weep and love,' and we rolled toward
the voice like one body and said
with our eyes closed, 'Then weep, then
love.' Buds of jasmine threaded through
her hair so they opened after dark,
brightening the room. That morning
rain as it would fall, still
falling, and where we had lain,
an arctic light steady
in the mind's releasing.

Black Pudding

Even then I knew it was the old unanswerable form of beauty
as pain, like coming onto a pair of herons
near the river mouth at dawn. Beauty as when the body
is a dumb stick before the moment – yet goes on,
gazes until memory prepares a quick untidy room
with unpredictable visiting hours.
So I brought you there, you who didn't belong, thinking to outsave
memory by tearing the sacred from

its alcove. I let you see us, arms helplessly tender,
holding each other all night on that awkward couch
because our life was ending. Again and again
retelling our love between gusts of weeping.
Did I let you overhear those gray-blue dyings?
Or as I think now, like a Mongol tribesman, did I stop the horse
on its desert march, take the meal of blood

from its bowed neck to be heated. This then is my black pudding
only the stalwart know to eat. How I climbed
like a damp child waking from nightmare to find
the parents intimate and still awake.
And with natural animal gladness, rubbed my face
into the scald of their cheeks, tasting salt
of the unsayable – but, like a rescuer who comes too late, too
fervently marked with duty, was unable to fathom

what their danger and passage had been for. Except
as you know now, to glimpse is intrusion enough,
and when there is nothing else to sustain, blood will be thickened
with fire. Not a pretty dish.
But something taken from the good and cherished beast on loan to us,
muscled over in spirit and strong enough to carry us
as far as it can, there being advantage
to this meagerness, unsavoriness that rations itself
and reminds us to respect even its bitter portion.
Don't ask me now why I'm walking my horse.

Now That I Am Never Alone

In the bath I look up and see the brown moth
pressed like a pair of unpredictable lips
against the white wall. I heat up
the water, running as much hot in as I can stand.
These handfuls over my shoulder – how once
he pulled my head against his thigh and dipped
a rivulet down my neck of coldest water from the spring
we were drinking from. Beautiful mischief
that stills a moment so I can never look
back. Only now, brightest now, and the water
never hot enough to drive that shiver out.

But I remember solitude – no other
presence and each thing what it was. Not this raw
fluttering I make of you as you have made of me
your watch-fire, your killing light.

Legend with Sea Breeze

When you died I wanted at least to ring
some bells, but there were only clocks
in my town and one emblematic clapper
mounted in a pseudo-park for veterans.
If there had been bells I would have
rung them, the way they used to sound
school bells in the country so children
in my mother's time seemed lit
from the other side with desire
as they ran in from the fields
with schoolbooks over their shoulders.
Once more a yellow infusion of bells

empties like a vat of canaries into
the heart so it is over-full and
the air stumbles above rooftops, and death
in its quicksilver-echo shakes
our marrow with a yellow, trilling
silence. I would have given you that,

though these nightshift workers,
these drinkers in childless taverns, these mothers
of daughters seduced at fourteen – what
can the language of bells say to them
they haven't known first as swallows
blunting the breastbone? No, better

to lead my black horse into that grove
of hemlock and stand awhile. Better
to follow it up Blue Mountain Road
and spend the day with sword ferns,
with the secret agitations of creaturely
forest-loneliness. Or to forage
like a heat-stunned bear
raking the brambles for berries and thinking
only winter, winter, and of crawling
in daylight into the beautiful excess of earth
to meet an equal excess of sleep.
Oh my black horse, what's

the hurry? Stop awhile. I want to carve
his initials into this living tree.
I'm not quite empty enough to believe he's gone,
and that's why the smell of the sea
refreshes these silent boughs, and why
some breath of him is added if I mar the ritual,
if I put utter blackness to use
so a tremor reaches him as hoofbeats, as
my climbing up onto his velvet shoulders
with only love, thunderous sea-starved love,
so in the little town where they lived
they won't exaggerate when they say
in their stone-colored voices

that a horse and a woman flew down
from the mountain, and their eyes looked out
the same, like the petals of black pansies
schoolchildren press into the hollow
at the base of their throats as a sign
of their secret, wordless invincibility.
Whatever you do, don't let them ring any bells.
I'm tired of schooling, of legends, of
those ancient sacrificial bodies dragged to death
by chariots. I just want to ride my black horse,
to see where he goes.

Souvenir

It is good to be unused, whole as discovery –
the alabaster egg with its giant stirring.
At first, with the heat gone out of me
I thought his moon-life had lifted everything
from reach, even roses, those vermilion climbers
that were a shout at hope, up and up
my haggard trellis. But goodness
has so many silent children whose spell
lifts anchors to vessels of rock and azure, and we
go happily under our black mantle
with a tingling inside as those who live close
to the weather delight in the plain grammar
of ice, of wind over fresh tracks
through the empty valley.

So she put on her birdskin moccasins
and went out to possess her island, making sure
the tide was at ebb. Drawn by doves, she
went out with his sickle over her
in the paradise-field of stars. Wet stones
that loved with their whole being are legion
on her shore. How blackly they shine, singed and frenzied
with memory, their birth-sheen
holding on. She would throw them all back
to add intention like that proud mouth
who, in mourning, saved her drinking
only for fountains. Lucina she calls herself
under his crown of candles, Lucina with her wedding cake
crumbled into the sea. What has she saved? Rue
and red ribbon, a wreath made of tail feathers.

As with her, an early death has left its pagan mark
so everything turns to worship or sign
and I am never more alone
than when our twin gold rings come together
in a perfect chime, addressing us in the familiar
lost-future tense. I stroke her glistening hair
as he stroked mine, absently, the way candlelight licks
the night clean until one of us is gone
or disheveled into a second soul.

II

*If we believe in the soul, then perhaps
we have more in common with the dead
than the living.*

JEFF KELLER
from a letter

Embers

He was suffering from too much light
the way our afternoons recover from
morning rain by slicing the room
in half. I read to him to bring a voice
sideways, to touch him more, and join
our listening or laughter or mutual derision.
To be one and none. Sometimes a rhyme can
snuff its substance, yet release
a second lasting. To speak aloud at a grave
breaks silence so another heat
shows through. Not speaking, but the glow
of that we spoke.

Two of Anything

What silk-thin difference is there
if I stay to dream or go.
KYOKO SELDEN

That small tug, which at first seems
all on its own in the strait,
can eventually be seen to pull two barges, each
twice its size, because water
understands everything and all
day says 'pass, pass by'. I propose
a plan and we discuss it. I'm afraid I'll never
be happy again. 'Bring me
a glass of water,' he says. 'Someone, you know,
has to stay here and take care of things.'
Two ducks fly by. I take
a few sips from his glass. Outside it's
deep blue morning, almost purple
it's so glad to be cheating
the sleepers of its willful drifting, the tangled
blue of night and the blue premonition
that will dissolve and carry
it. Two boys vicious with news fling
the morning paper house to house
down the hill. Two horses out of childhood I loved,
Daisy and Colonel Boy, are hitched
to the wagon. I hear the cold extravagance of
tiny bells welded into their harness straps.
Iron wheels under us over snow
for miles through the walnut groves. The two
pearled hair combs he gave me
make a chilly mouth on the sill. I look up and out
over water at the horizon – no, two
horizons. One reached and entered with him, and so
is under me, and the other
far enough away to be the dead mate of this one.
Between them, lively passage of boats, none
empty. That's fascinating,
I said to the poet, let me add one. I thought
there was more water in this glass.
I guess not, one of us said.

Sad Moments

That less than torment you lived so fully –
now at least it's possible
to make it functional, the way a chopping block
becomes a footstool once the heads
have rolled. But it gives you no
rest, his holding the stem
of that Japanese maple into the hole
and saying, 'Even this thing is going to outlive
me.' Tamping the dirt
down with both hands, making sure. Or when,
at the airport in Reno, he came back
glazed over from blowing all his loose change, yours
too – that worse than woeful grin,
cocksure in its lastness, so to smile back was
the less-than-answer needed. 'That's the last slot
I'll ever play, I guess.' And remembering isn't

to cling, any more than he did, but to acknowledge
no one can die in those moments
either, moments vaulted like a cave with seepage
and echo so they outlive what makes you
forget – those little economies
of the blood that stunt the attention until
the scent of lilac or pitch gets
manageable again and we are fit for modulation and
whim, for cloves and lace, or
that dim creaturely train rushing past us with one
darkened car where nothing but applause
can be heard, and not to know
what it's for, or if its black intoxication
will somehow empty out those raw strips
of night, freshen them
so someone later can lie down for a while,
vulnerable as he was, milder at the end than sleep.

Ring

Not the one he's wearing in that stopped length
of ground, but the one we saw together
in the little shop in Oregon – moss agate so green
it was nearly black on its silver band. Hard
to come across it after, emptied of his hand
and watchful. Thinking to surprise its power
with treason, I gave it to our friend who wore
no rings and needed its luck. But soon I knew,
don't ask me how, the ring
lay among lesser things in a drawer. I asked

for it back, and for a while, wore it on a chain
around my neck. But it was awkward
like a high-school charm, the sign of love a girl
outgrows – not as it was, exchanged for the rose-gold
of wedding bands. Where is it now?
In some abject safety.
But where? Put away. I turn the house upside down
searching. Not to find it – worse
than omen. Like happiness squandered in fountains
with wrongheaded wishing. Or the hit-and-miss

taunt of memory, its dulled signature so casual
it crushes me lucid and I believe what I don't believe
in the way of true apparitions – that he uses
my longing to call himself to me,
that my senses are inhabited like the log
into which a bear has crawled to dream
winter away, that the ongoing presence of the dead
is volatile, sacramental. The wind he's
attached to – that boy, running with a kite over
the gravestones, looking up, keeping his footing

as if he worked sky into the earth with
a cool boldness. So the dead-aliveness of my love
turns in the flux of memory, of what his memory
would recall, as he is recalled
to a street in Oregon, dead and alive in love,
with the strangeness of cold silver
close around the finger on his new-made hand.

He Would Have

To speak for him is to leave a breath
pulled suddenly from an overlapping realm
suspended in the room. So this morning
snow lightly cupped in salal is raised against
the hillside by fresh ardor alone
because he would have called to me
while putting on the morning coffee
to look out and see it into its island moment,
spiraled double and darkly inward
by our pushing pleasure up another notch
until the world stays as beneficent as it is.
I stand at the window the better to amplify
cool underneath of petals a snow-lit green.
Any unexpected bounty adds him like seasoning
to the day, as when the eagle uses the frayed
sky-green of the neighboring hemlock to
beguile our paired attentions, his white head
at its topped crown washed clean of the past and
                    the future.
                    Alert raw knot of infinity.

Thieves at the Grave

Now snow has fallen I have been to you
in all weather, especially lovebird weather,
a valence throughout, thanks to
the viewpoint at the cliff edge
where teenagers park to rehearse in daylight
certain suppressions of desire
so as to repeal them more aggressively
at dark. Their glances along the shore below
and farther out at the fishing boats reflect a gauze
of homecoming as when your patina of green
wears through me. Purposeful

then to bury you above our fishing grounds.
Purposeful as fish locked in their fluidity,
as we are. Location, says the snow,
is what you do to me, what I record briefly
and change into second nature. My knee-marks
are two bald companion moons where we glide
grassily in place. I leave things
to test your company – the two potted plants
so tempting in August bees were a fever
in goldenrod and I could think, 'He loves
their industry.' By September someone
had hefted them away into a secret garden.
That simple desecration, the thief's prerogative,

joined you back to my living, and we are benefactors
to shepherds, blind walkers, a braille of winds.
What the bees took they gave again
to flowers as much caressed as we were.
But those glassed-in kisses
with their motors running are edged
by another snow: how did we live so well before
with nothing missing?

Cold Crescent

Walking idly through the shops on the wharf
while waiting for the ferry to take us
across – we don't know yet
you are dying. But I hold that black shawl so long,
admiring lace against flesh, the way it enhances me cold
like bird song over snow, partial
and what we vanish from. So you were unafraid and
offered to buy it for me. And neither of us
noticed overmuch as money was paid
and into my hands it was
delivered, a simple swath of cloth.

I remember taking it freshly
out of the drawer, the crispness of black, its
breaking off at both ends into daylight, as death
breaks us off or shouts into itself
until a tingling ambushes the room and it is all we can do
not to follow that swoop of not-coming-backness.

But I'm past that now, as the crescent moon says
of its full stony profile. Tonight the moon is blond.
His sideways light bends inward to cheat
the dark. That's why he's here, to hand me
the white shawl knitted beside some missing fire.
When he sets it across my shoulders
I am lowered gently down
and made to sleep again on earth.

After the Chinese

By daybreak a north wind has shaken
the snow from the fir boughs. No disguise
lasts long. Did you think there were no winds
under the earth? My Tartar horse prefers
a north wind. Did you think
a little time and death would stop me?
Didn't you choose me for the stubborn
set of my head, for green eyes that dared
the cheat and the haggler from our door?
I've worn a little path, an egg-shaped circle
around your grave keeping warm
while I talk to you. I'm the only one
in the graveyard. You chose well. No one
is as stubborn as me, and my Tartar horse
prefers a north wind.

III

THE VALENTINE ELEGIES

In love longing
I listen to the monk's bell.
I will never forget you
even for an interval
short as those between
the bell notes.

IZUMI SHIKIBU

The Burning Heart:
Women Poets of Japan
translated and edited by
Kenneth Rexroth and Ikuko Atsumi

Black Valentine

I run the comb through his lush hair,
letting it think into my wrist
the way the wrist whispers to the cards
with punctuation and savvy in a game of solitaire.
So much not to be said the scissors
are saying in the hasp and sheer
of the morning. Eleven years I've cut
his hair and even now, this last time, we hide
fear to save pleasure
as bulwark. *My dearest* – the hair says as it brushes my
thighs – *my only* – on the way to the floor. If the hair
is a soul-sign, the soul obeys our gravity, piles up
in animal mounds and worships the feet. We're
silent so peace rays over us like Bernice's hair
shaken out across the heavens. If there were gods
we are to believe they animated her shorn locks
with more darkness than light, and harm
was put by after the Syrian campaign, and
harm was put by as you tipped the cards
from the table like a child bored
with losing. I spread my hair like a tent over us
to make safety wear its twin heads, one to face death,
the other blasted so piteously by love
you throw the lantern of the moment against
the wall and take me in with our old joke, the one
that marks my northern skies, 'Hey, babe,' you say
like a man who knows how to live on earth. 'Hey,'
with your arm around my hips, 'what you doing
after work?' Silly to ask now if the hair
she put on the altar, imagining her power over
his passage, was dead or living.

Quiver

I am even younger now than you, for a while,
in the way his early death has scraped away my future
so I have nowhere else to go but back, back
to youth, my schoolgirl heart! How it likes to leap, to
throw itself away, tossing the heads off
pansies from a height to let the butterfly come out.
'What more?' it asks, not 'how
long?' 'Take off your blouse,' he says in his hilarious
English, your cardiologist friend from Prague. 'Miro,
say *unbutton* your blouse, please.' Already he bends – 'They're not
easy, these buttons.' Such
a beautiful word, *buttons*, when he said
it. Glad for lace to reward him, Miro with his ear to
his stethoscope to my heart, my breast-beat. We are not

twins tonight – you on the couch with your faulty pulse.
Mine is hiding out, refusing to
click. It knows time has no arrow, only suddenness and
yearning, its savage two-edged smile transfigured by
command. I hand you the ivory chopsticks – my hair tumbles
down. It always does when I drink sake, when my hands go
China white. So it isn't remembering, but silver and exact
when I tell Miro of my lost jazz-playing friend, lost
in Prague Spring in 1968, Milosz who loved to kiss
standing up with his hands against my shoulder blades, Milosz
who did not hitchhike to Paris, but disappeared into Prague as a
stone enters well water, though he sent recorded Christmas carols
the second Christmas we never saw each other again. Love gets

younger like that, remembering what didn't happen, younger
and more uniquely desolate, the way youngest love
wants to be rid of ornamentation, to shed, to clasp, to stroke
the wrong way until the skin roars. Miro, whose sleep
I have stolen in my vague lethargy of rain-held
amours, armors, my graceful hinges. What
can he think, snapping his fingers and dancing alone
in the cramped bedroom to the radio's callow
vigor, as we put the book of the moon aside so its crescent
wavers in its cycle of harvest – vessel in which
the shadow of the rabbit is drowned, in which a shuddering
moves its whimsical bohemian soul across the sounds made of

me and I am younger than you have ever been, like a shelter
built from branches by children who will wade the river
and forget, carrying their snowy elbows
like rudders through the current with their mouths
open, as mine is open, and his lips not even lips
they are so far from living, my hair parted
at the neck where his eyelids close, so moonstone, so
borrowed from what I knew of that innocent heart, ghosted now.
As this is kindness, not love, to let the girl
have something to replace, to replay
like false acacias or an artificial lake. Still as luxury
she keeps and keeps, and is a grove carefully
worked upon.

Fresh Stain

I don't know now if it was kindness – we do
and we do. But I wanted you with me
that day in the cool raspberry vines, before
I had loved anyone, when another girl and I
saw the owner's son coming to lift away
our heaped flats of berries. His
white shirt outside his jeans so
tempting. That whiteness, that quick side-glance
in our direction. We said nothing,
but quickly gathered all the berries we could, losing
some in our mirth and trampling them
like two black ponies who only want to keep their backs
free, who only want to be shaken with
the black night-in-day murmur of hemlocks
high above. Our slim waists, our buds
of breasts and red stain of raspberries cheapening
our lips. We were sudden, we were
two blurred dancers who didn't need paradise. His shirt,
his white shirt when the pelting ended, as if
we had kissed him until his own blood
opened. So we refused every plea and
were satisfied. And you didn't touch me then, just
listened to the cool silence after. Inside,

the ripe hidden berries as we took up our wicker baskets
and lost our hands past the wrists
in the trellised vines. Just girls with the arms of
their sweaters twisted across their hips, their laughter
high in sunlight and shadow, that girl
you can almost remember as she leans into the vine,
following with pure unanswerable desire, a boy
going into the house to change his shirt.

Rain-soaked Valentine

As if some child, unwilling to shut even
the figurative heart into pocket or
lunch pail, had carried it plate-like
home in a downpour. A passionate
migration – no matter its redundant shape
and thirty others just as crude. The passage
did it good, white lace bleeding, the stock
message smudged out of language by rivulets
and soaring. It came with a lunge,
earnestness of moment, refusing
to be merely 'sufficient' as in prudent love –
the effect gauged before the gift.
Anciently worn to trash on its way to me, it
doesn't care if I am moonlight. Just arriving
is candor, is courting.

Crazy Menu

Last of his toothpaste, last of his Wheat Chex, last
of his 5-Quick-Cinnamon-Rolls-With-Icing, his
Pop Secret Microwave Pop-
corn, his Deluxe Fudge Brownie Mix next to my
Casbah Nutted Pilaf on the sparser
shelf. I'm using it all up. Chanting: he'd-want-me-
to-he'd-want-me-to. To consume loss like a hydra-headed
meal of would-have-dones accompanied by
missed-shared-delight. What can I tell you?
I'm a lost proof.
But something eats with me, a darling of
the air-that-is. It smacks its unkissable lips and
pours me down with a gleam in its unblinkable eye, me –
the *genius loci* of his waiting room to this feast of rapidly
congealing unobtainables. Oh-me-of-
the-last-of-his-lastness through which I am gigantically
left over like the delight of Turkish

Delight. Don't haul out your memory vault to
cauterize my green-with-moment-thumb. Or shove me
into the gloom-closet of yet another cannibalistic
Nevermore. I've been there. And there too. It was not
unusual – that bravado of a castrato in a brothel
yanking his nose and waxing paradisal. No, I'm more like
a Polish miner who meets a Chinese miner at a
helmet convention in Amsterdam. Because we both
speak a brand of Philip Morris English picked up
from a now extinct murmur heard only impromptu
at a certain caved-in depth, we are overwhelmed by
the sheer fact of meeting and we clasp
each other by our bare heads for nights, exchanging
the unimpoverishable secrets of the earth, the going down and
the coming up, the immutable pretext of light, a common history
of slumped canaries, of bereaved kinfolk, of black-lunged
singers and handmade coffins. We trade
a few eulogies and drinking songs and sit down at last to
a huge meal of aged cheese and kippers.
We lean into our vitals

with all the lights off. It's dark inside and out.
This is our last chance to revel in the unencumbered
flickering of Balinese tapers we bought at
a souvenir stand above the canal. Like rice and spit
we are tolerant of all occasions, this being
the lifting of the dread whereby
the girls' wings we autograph onto our duffle coats
have been painted like butterflies, only
on the upside so the dark is mocked by
our raised arms, our fluttered concentration, uncollectable as
the lastness I am of him I love-ed
scribbled unsentimentally on a valentine in 1983:
> *To the King of my Heart!*
In daylight we pick up our tinned rations and hike off,
every artery and nerve of us, into the rest
of our commemorative lives.

Posthumous Valentine

You want me to know I'm keeping memories
so you unlatch a few. The future's
in there too, badly restrained
like an actress so intently fastened on
her cue: 'pocketknife' – she stumbles out
on 'doctor's wife' and, mistaken
for the maid, is chased out so as not
to interrupt the kiss. But that's already in
the past. I remember how nicely stingy
they were – streamlining my impromptu
intervals like a serious canoe just
composed enough for two.

Strange Thanksgiving

I don't know anyone at the table except
the friend who's brought me, who knows only
the host and hostess. I perch on my chair
like an egret, snowy and attentive. The man
to my left is the youngest son of an onion farmer.
The crop this year was ruined by rain.
His wrist is speckled blue from painting his
girlfriend's Chevy last night. We talk
about his hobby, building underwater cars. He
drove one off a dock into a lake. Nice
to putt around under the ducks, then wheel
on shore and go for burgers. Our host

draws up a chair, offers three kinds of pie.
He plays vicious squash to stay ahead of his bad
back. His wife will be near-dead
on the bathroom floor from swallowing pills
a few short nights away. But things
are holding now. Even that crumb at the edge of
my friend's mouth. I reach up
as if we're man and wife and brush it
away, unconscious tenderness letting my hand
graze for a moment my own love's face
and so, submerged, fall heavily to sea in the homely
clatter of plates lifted suddenly

away. We're stalled out and anxious
in the chitchat before the hearth. Soon
into our coats and thank-yous. Getting to the car
down a fresh bank of snow, I steady myself
on my friend's sure grip. The ride home is better
than sleep, initialled over with afterthoughts we speak
out loud in that half-heard, half-said way – yet easy
to feel rescued by his debonair steering through
the unacknowledged coma of side streets. His intimacy
to know I'm beyond accompaniment and already
home, dividing myself with approach
like two moon-bright windows, seen after dark, across a field.

Meeting Beyond Meeting

There is threat of you here as the sea
shows its blackest hour before nightfall,
then doubles back to take it all.
But for a while the trees are silhouetted
against a band of shaggy lavender across
a bridge of pink-edged light.
I could still believe the door will open
and you will be standing there,
a little surprised I'm not with
anyone yet.

Now the light's extinguished
and we who knew every curve and dip and scar
must claim each other like hands picking orchids
in the dark. We can tell only by the fragrance
how much needs crushing.

Magenta Valentine

Today my love feels Italian, reminiscent of
blood spilled between the Austrian and
Franco-Sardinian armies at Magenta, bluer and
deeper than Harvard crimson. Captain Caprilli is
yet to be born to instruct the cavalry.
The rider is still an encumbrance to the horse.
I drink espresso in the little café with its back to
the harbor, try to think of you with other
than longing, more like a very old and mostly forgotten
battle that haunts a few leftover war brides
who eventually married somebody living.
My heart surges blackly. Knows other likelihoods.

Valentine Delivered by a Raven

Its beak is red and it has a battlefield-look,
as if it's had its pickings and come away
of its own volition. Elsewhere the Emperor Frederick
sleeps on, guarded by ravens, and may yet rise
from deathly slumber and walk the earth.
Who knows what's long enough
when death's involved. I stand on my love's grave
and say aloud in a swoop of gulls
over the bay, 'I kiss your lips, babe,' and it's not
grotesque, even though the mind knows what it
knows, and mostly doesn't. Language,
that great concealer, is more than generous, gives
always what it doesn't have. I stare into the dazzling
impertinent eye of the messenger. He's
been tending the dead so long his eyes are garnets,
his wings cracked open to either side, two
fissures savage with light. I bend
in recognition and take up a holly bough left
as in the old adornment of doorways. The hard, red
berries glisten and tremble in their nest of
green, so when he speaks I hear him
with the attention of a red berry before a covetous
bright eye, and what I need I take
in empires before he flaps away on my love's errands
and I am cinnabar and fog in the doorway.

IV

And this holy man of great directness
and simplicity, big white teeth shining,
laughs out loud in an infectious way
at Jang-bu's question. Indicating his twisted legs
without a trace of self-pity or bitterness, as if
they belonged to all of us, he casts his arms wide
to the sky and the snow mountains, the high sun
and dancing sheep, and cries, 'Of course I am happy here!
It's wonderful! Especially
when I have no choice!'

PETER MATTHIESSEN
The Snow Leopard

Paradise

Morning and the night uncoupled.
My childhood friend
who had been staying awake for me, left the house
so I could be alone with the powerful raft of his body.

He seemed to be there only for listening, an afterlife
I hadn't expected. So I talked to him, told him
things I needed to hear myself
tell him, and he listened, I can say 'peacefully,'
though maybe it was only an effect he had, the body's surety
when it becomes one muscle. Still, I believe I heard
my own voice then, as he might have heard it, eagerly
like the nostrils of any mare blowing softly over
the damp presence he was, telling it
all is safe here, all is calm and yet to be endured
where you are gone from.

I spoke until there was nothing unfinished between us.
Since his feet were still there and my hands
I rubbed them with oil
because it is hard to imagine at first
that the dead don't enjoy those same things they did
when alive. And even if it happened only as a last thing, it
was the right last thing.

For to confirm what is forever beyond speech
pulls action out of us. And if it is only childlike and
unreceived, the way a child hums to the stick
it is using to scratch houses into the dirt, still
it is a silky membrane and shining
even to the closed eye.

Ebony

I need these dark waves pulsing in my sleep.
How else make up for the pungency
of that carnation's breath freshened over us,
night on night? Just to lie next to love
was to have the garden in all its seasons.
I see that now. Gently, and without
the false luster of pain meant to tempt
memory into crushed fragrance.
In the pull and toss of stones below the house
a soothing spirit sifts and laves its weights,
and those that were tears in some oriental legend
are strongly effaced in the wearing. You,
who were only a stone, taught stone to me in aftermath.
Which is to mock containment at its rich periphery.
The gray, the green in my black.

Fathomless

The peacock has eaten the poison orchid
and shakes poison into beauty of feathers as
easily as my hair unlatches its
black hairpins into the pool
the sunken grave has made of him.
They drop and drop.
From a long way off I hear them strike bone
that could be eye-socket or pelvis or
sternum. The sound is not what I
expected. Not the startled gold
of his wedding band. Not that. More
the soft plinging of arrows shot
in a dream toward my own face, stopped there,
above a pool where someone else's tears
have broken unruly, and fall softly
through the eye.

Breeze

Don't you think I'm tired of tragedy?
It's not even my word. Not theirs either
when they apply that ghost-talcum
to us. We're comic-strip. Kill one
of us and a legion of lovers
steps forward. You spring to life because
what else can I call it when you
soar into me like a cheerleader marooned
in a meadow. I shake my crepe tassels.
How happily they rustle, tossed there
on the tall grass.

Deaf Poem

Don't read this one out loud. It isn't
to be heard, not even in the sonic zones
of the mind should it trip the word 'explosion'
and detonate in the silent room. My love
needs a few words that stay out of
the mouth and vocal cords. No vibrations, please.
He needs to put his soul's freshly inhuman capacity
into scattering himself deeper into
the forest. It's part of the plan that birds
will eat the markings. It's okay. He's not coming
that way again. He likes it where he is. Or if he
doesn't, I can't know anything about it. Let
the birds sing. He always liked to hear them
any time of day. But let this poem meet
its deafness. It pays attention another way, like he
doesn't when I bow my head and press my forehead
in the swollen delusion of love's power to
manifest across distance the gladness that joined us.

Wherever he is he still knows I have two feet
and one of them is broken from dancing.
He'd come to me if he could. It's nice to be sure
of something when speaking of the dead. Sometimes
I forget what I'm doing and call out to him. It's me! How
could you go off like that? Just as things were
getting good. I'm petulant, reminding him of his promise
to take me in a sleigh pulled by horses
with bells. He looks back in the dream – the way
a violin might glance across a room at its bow
about to be used for kindling. He doesn't
try to stop anything. Not the dancing. Not the deafness
of my poems when they arrive like a sack of wet
stones. Yes, he can step back into life just long enough
for eternity to catch hold, until one of us
is able to watch and to write the deaf poem,
a poem missing even the language
it is unwritten in.

We're All Pharaohs When We Die

Our friends die with us
  and the sky too
    in huge swatches, and lakes, and places
      we walked past, just going and
        coming.
The spoons we ate with look dim, a little deadened
  in the drawer. Their trips to the mouth
    forlorn, and the breath caught there
      fogged to a pewtery smudge.

Our friends die with us and are thrown in because we
used them so well.
But they also stay on earth awhile like the abandoned
  huts of the Sherpas on a mountain that doesn't know
    it's being climbed. They don't fall down all at once.
      Not like his heart
fell down, dragging
the whole gliding eternity of him out of sight.

Guttural and aslant, I chew the leather sleeve
  of his jacket, teething like a child on the unknown pressure
    budding near its tongue. But the tongue
      is thrown in too, everyone's who said his name
as he used to be called
in our waking and sleeping,
  dreaming and telling the dreams.
    Yes, the dreams are thrown in
so the mystery
  breaks through still wearing its lid, and I am never
    to be seen again
      out of his muslin striding.

If this is my lid then, with its eyebrows painted on, with its
stylized eyes glazed open above the yet-to-be-dead ones, even so
  a dead-aliveness looks through
    as trees are thrown in
      and clouds and the meadows under the orchards
the deer like to enter – those returning souls
  who agree to be seen
    gazing out of their forest-eyes
with our faint world painted over them.

V

One day a monk came to the master, Yoshu, at a monastery in the mountains. Upon arriving, the monk asked: 'This place is very well-known for its natural stone bridge that is said to span the rapids, but as I come here I don't see any stone bridge. I see only a rotten piece of board, a plank. Where is your bridge, pray tell me, O master?'

The master now answered in this way: 'You see only that miserable, rickety plank and don't see the stone bridge?'

The disciple said: 'Where is the stone bridge then?'

And the master answered him: 'Horses pass over it, donkeys pass over it, cats and dogs, tigers and elephants pass over it, men and women, the poor and the rich, the young and the old, the humble and the noble, Englishmen, perhaps Japanese, Muslims, Christians; spirituality and materiality, the ideal and the practical, the supreme and the most commonplace things. They all pass over it. Even you, O monk, pass over it.'

DAISETZ TEITARO SUZUKI
The Awakening of Zen

'Said Jesus, on whom be peace: The world is a bridge, pass over it, but build no house there.'

Inscription on Akbar's Gate of Victory

Moon Crossing Bridge

If I stand a long time by the river
when the moon is high
don't mistake my attention
for the merely aesthetic, though
that saves in daylight.
Only what we once called worship
has feet light enough to carry
the living on that span of brightness.
And who's to say I didn't cross
just because I used the bridge in its witnessing,
to let the water stay the water
and the incongruities of the moon to chart
that joining I was certain of.

Spacious Encounter

What they cut away in braids from childhood
returns. I use it. With my body's nearest silk
I cover you in the dream-homage, attend and revive
by attending. I know very little of what to do
without you. Friends say, 'Go on with your life.'
But who's assigned this complicitous extension,
these word-caressings? this night-river
full of dead star-tremors, amazed floatings, this
chaotic laboratory of broken approaches?

Your unwritten pages lift an ongoing dusk in me.
Maybe this makes me your only reader now. The one
you were writing towards all along, who can't put down
her double memory pressed to shape
your one bodiless body. Book I am wearing in my night-rushing
to overtake these kneelings and contritions of daylight. Book
that would be a soul's reprisal
if souls could abandon their secret missions
so necessary to our unbelief. No,
the embrace hasn't ended.
Though everyone's grief-clock
runs down. Even mine sweeps
the room and goes forth with a blank face
more suited each day to enduring.

Ours is the compressed altitude
of two beings who share one retina
with the no-world seared onto it, and
the night-river rushing through, one-sided,
and able to carry what is one-sidedly felt
when there is no surface to what
flows into you. Embrace
I can't empty. Embrace I would know with my arms
cut away on no street in no universe
to which we address so much unprofound silence.
I unshelter you – my vanishing
dialogue, my remnant, my provision.

Anniversary

If the sun could walk into a room
you would not dare to want
such a man as he. But blindness
has prepared me, is requisite
to love put away, like breath
put away from the half-opened mouth,
breath that returns, withdraws,
returns again. As he does
and does not.

We ate the wedding feast quietly
and to ourselves near the hush
of the gaming tables, the icy click
of dice in the half-closed hand
before they are thrown.
There were no toasts to the future
because by then it was a day
about to begin, which
was already stunted
by the hazard of its own
oblivion. What could I tell you
of love at that moment
that would be simple and true enough
since words are candles I blow out
the moment I set them down?
Better to scrape wax from the table edge
with a fingernail. Better to stare
into the eye of a horse
brought to drink from the mouth
of a river where it opens
into the sea. All was liquid
and tranquil there, and though our lips
were kept from touching
by the great sleep of space
before us, everything poured into us
hard and true, and when we set our glasses
down, the darkness of the horse's
overflowing eye closed over us.

I Stop Writing the Poem

to fold the clothes. No matter who lives
or who dies, I'm still a woman.
I'll always have plenty to do.
I bring the arms of his shirt
together. Nothing can stop
our tenderness. I'll get back
to the poem. I'll get back to being
a woman. But for now
there's a shirt, a giant shirt
in my hands, and somewhere a small girl
standing next to her mother
watching to see how it's done.

Cherry Blossoms

Chekhov wanting to write about 'the wave of
child suicides sweeping across Russia' – plunged
by that sentence into sudden pity for
myself and my three brothers growing up,
as my father had, under the strap. Pity
for my father who worked and slept, worked
and drank and was the dispenser of woe.
Our child bodies learning despair, learning to quake
and cower – the raw crimson of pain given by
the loving hand. No wonder, for a while,

animals drew close to us, as if our souls
overlapped. And so we died there. And were
attended by animals. One dog especially
I remember with brightest gratitude.
Miles of night and her wild vowellings under
great moons, subsiding into a kind of atrocious
laughter, what I think of now as faint gleams
of demoniac nature ratifying itself. Somehow

that viewless dread she recorded seared
my childhood with survival – she who
was mercifully and humbly buried somewhere
with a little *sotoba* over her, bearing the unnecessary
text: 'Even within such as this animal,
    the Knowledge Supreme will enfold at last.'
               And so my old friend died.

And the cherry blossoms fell sumptuously.
And I wrote a little *sotoba* in my determined
              child-hand, to insure that never again
could they be put back
                    onto our bare branches.

Knotted Letter

It seems to me, though, that you always
understand very well what I can't say very well.
HARUKI MURAKAMI
A Wild Sheep Chase

There is that getting worse at saying
that comes from being understood
in nuance, because the great illiteracy
of rain keeps writing over my days
as if to confirm the possibility
of touching everything so it glistens
with its bliss bent aside by some soft
undirected surpassing.

I say to the never-injured creature:
the shears have rent my silk – unsolving
beauty, hard and bright – until I am so consequent
with time it is accomplice
and spills neither backwards nor
forwards. I ask him to live by miscalculation
my capricious scheme. Counsel him to miss light
an oar's moment and be ocean-cold
as love's splashing after-touch, the blade-edge
actual, but under spell
and scarlet to what it gladly slips
as a thing too near and precious – a shadowy fish
drowsy with the overgarment of planets and stars
it haunts below, as if to commemorate
the unseen by the marbled distortions
guessed at. Because the kisses come mixed with sand
and we know the mouth is full of strange, unwieldy
sediment. And because the samurai image of a sword
is thrust through clouds with only the hilt
showing, its unglinting edges like words
slashed to stubble where the wheat was gathered.

And this a gleaning twisted to the leafless bush
he was sure to pass, thinking by memory
her waist-length hair, her spoken face
as he would never see it, in the words
of poems so keenly obscured
the poem was her only face.

I Put On My New Spring Robe

Yamato Takeru-no-Mikoto, samurai hero of the Kojiki,
who 'turned into a white bird upon his death'.
No accident then, the headstone
to your left reads 'White' and the one chiseled
to your right is 'Bird.' – A man who could arrange this,
not knowing where he would be buried, has to be scary.

I burn cones of incense and watch the sweet smoke
drift across our faces. Yesterday when someone
asked how I was doing I laughed
like a woman whose fate is to sleep next to a sword.
Whitebird, that's what I call you in my dreams of flying.

Northwest by Northwest

Our stones are subtle here, a lavender that is
almost gray, a covert green
a step shy of its blue.
For eating, as with loneliness, we prefer
the bowl to the plate, for its
heaping up, its shapeliness of offering
what it half encloses. Just
when it seems the day has gone to sleep, the eagle
drops suddenly from its black chambers.

The silks of drowsy weddings sham the horizon and ecstasy
is a slow mirage we drift towards, voyaging in
some eternal orient whose seasons
ache, serenely inhabit, but disdain
to yield. The *she* who rules here leans
across the void to reward our perpetual suspension
with an ongoing tomb – 'If,' she says, 'you
existed.' Requiring pleasure to revolve
outside its answer.

Picking Bones

Emiko here from Tokyo in her red dress
and voice like a porcelain hand
on silk. We carry roses to the grave
under the tilt of gulls. Some have
walked their hieroglyphics across the poem
carved there, to make sure we comprehend
this stopping off to flight. Small tasks

prepare another silence, kinship of pouring
water, fallen petals brushed across granite.
Gradually we come there after we've
come there. Hard to light candles
in the breeze from the strait. His delight
flickers and gusts. We are steady
and erased a little more. Finally we talk quietly,

the presence palpable as we crouch there.
That overlay too of new sound Emiko has given
his poems in Japanese. Our voices nudge closer
on the cliffside. Pungency and sweetness
of joss sticks, Emiko says, in Japanese cemeteries,
and smoke curling up. After cremation of the loved one,
working in pairs, the relatives join in the ritual

of 'picking bones'. Two by two with chopsticks lifting
each bone from the ashes, dropping it
into an urn. Her friend, Yoshi, who said he had
much feeling and grief on viewing
his father's body, but who saw and felt,
in lifting shards of a father – the lightness, the necessary
discrepancy of translation. For a moment we are held

precariously as a morsel
on the way to any mouth. 'Don't
pick bones!' the mothers warn children caught
lifting the same piece of food. We pull
ourselves up from the low black table, from
                              the ivory clicking.

Blue Grapes

Eating blue grapes
        near the window
    and looking out
        at the snow-covered valley.
For a moment, the deep world
        gazing back. Then a blue jay
    scatters snow from a bough.
No world, no meeting. Only
        tremors, sweetness
                on the tongue.

At The-Place-of-Sadness

I take a photo of the stone Buddha
gazing from its eternal moment over
the eroded bodies of hundreds of child-sized
Buddhas. Shoulder to shoulder
they say something about death
not to be offered another way. The spirits
of those with no relatives to mourn them, an entity
driving tears inward so the face wears only the gust,
the implosion of grief.

Through the starred red of maple leaves: a man
half-visible in white shirt and black tie
held on a level with the stone Buddha – the one
in its living stillness, the other more-than-living
so he takes a step toward me
when I press the shutter ·
and glance up
like one of the dead
given the task of proving, with two identical stones,
the difference between
a spirit and a body.

Close to Me Now

Through low valley mist
I saw the horses
barely moving, caressed flank
and forelock, the dip
of the back. Human love is a wonder
if only to say: this body! the mist!

A Dusky Glow at Glenstaughey

Hefting turf onto the cart
in the long light, Helen's son Ricardo
gone home. Sufficiency of women's arms
in that old necessity of wars and rain. Mary
stacking the load as we swing the sacks up – good
use of knees to boost the heavier ones
into place. The air still and
brackish, pulling us close
on the hillside. Angela, forgetful in her
silk blouse, brought to the work
so suddenly her white is magnet to the scuff
of earth, the heels of her palms, like ours, etched
with the fine black of secret fire
the earth had been saving.

We ride the bonfire to the cottage yard
to stack the winter's heat. The flickering red
of cockscombs yet to bloom brushes the tractor wheels
to either side. How light
the earth is between us. Strange we are
in the blue air that stores its night.
Strange, like figures crowded off the edge
of memory.

Infinite Room

Having lost future with him
I'm fit now to love those
who offer no future when future
is the heart's way of throwing itself away
in time. He gave me all, even
the last marbled instant, and not as excess,
but as if a closed intention were itself
a spring by the roadside
I could put my lips to and be quenched
remembering. So love in a room now
can too easily make me lost
like a child having to hurry home
in darkness, afraid the house
will be empty. Or just afraid.

Tell me again how this is only
for as long as it lasts. I want to be
fragile and true as one who extends
the moment with its death intact,
with her too wise heart
cleansed of that debris we called hope.
Only then can I revisit that last surviving
and know with the wild exactness
of a shattered window what he meant
with all time gone
when he said, 'I love you.'

Now offer me again
what you thought was nothing.

Two Locked Shadows

Their joining is the way a buried self
exerts its chill in order to ravish
the greater light around it.
Like me, they cannot see what love loses
in being useless, but can feel
its certain gain. I will be poor
as darkness is to night
watching them in my soft hunger.
Where does her shoulder end or
the blue sparks thrown off
by his chest begin? My eyes
make up their grandeur
from a shapeless swelling, a clashing
without movement
that belongs to happiness
and signifies: only the body
is generous, is strong enough
to live past the sugary, hunchbacked claims
of the soul. The double cinch of
their sex draws my stepping through
like a sudden dart of pain
or joy, impossible to know which,
since whatever happens, when I step
into sunlight, they have kissed
my white cheekbones
expressionless.

Glow

Those Japanese women waiting, waiting
all the way back to Shikibu and Komachi
for men who, even then, seemed capable
of scant affection. Traitorous though,
not to admire the love of women
that shines down long corridors of the past
as steadily as those lanterns
I walked under beside the shrines of Kyōto.
Women who waited in vain, or to have sorrow
freshened by a cursory reappearance.
Their hope of meeting even a poor love again
gave each heart its rigorous vanishing.

Even a beautiful waste is waste.
Someone should have stepped through
the cobwebs in their pitiful doorways
with a new message: 'Not the work of love
but love itself, nothing less.'
That at least might have emptied
them sufficiently
to carry expectation past
its false chance at fulfillment.
Which is to say – when no right love came
they would not have been ready.
Something close at hand
would have claimed their attentions.

So I walked out one night under the full moon
and agreed with my dead love
that the cold light on the backs of my hands
belonged most to me.

VI

He holds me. Rainbows everywhere. What is more like a
rainbow than tears? Rain, a curtain, denser
than beads. I don't know if such embankments can
end. But here is a bridge and

> *— Well then?*

MARINA TSVETAYEVA
Poem of the End
translated by Elaine Feinstein

Un Extraño

Light begins. Snow begins.
A rose begins to unhinge
its petals. Sleep
begins. An apple lets go
of its branch. Someone tells
a secret like an echo
wrapped around a shadow,
a shadow soaked in love.
The secret begins to make
a difference. It travels
on the borrowed heat
of what the shadow
passes over. The lip
begins its mustache.
The heart begins its
savage journey
toward love and loss
of love. But you, you
don't begin. I stare
at your hand on my breast.
Their dialogue is the wingless
strength of the stem
bearing its flower
in rain, in sun.

Day begins. Night begins.
But you don't begin.
You know that one thing
the loveless lovers forget,
that to begin is to agree
to live among half-forces,
to shine only when the moon
shines and all is ready.

You make me ready
but you do not begin.
I let you never begin.
It's my gift to our most uncertain
always. I agree only to coincide
outside each death-enchanted
wave. What we are making
isn't a shroud or a halo.

It's a banished hive
stinging itself alive with
vast multiplications. We taunt love
as the bullfighter taunts
death, preparing the dangerous lunge
until it catches us unawares
that split second
in which love shudders
its starkest glimpse
into us. The magenta cape
swirls its silk across our lips
like a breath unravelled in the moment
the matador kneels to the bull.
My *adorno, el novillito*. Don't
begin. Don't ever begin.

Incomprehensibly

Because we have chosen them
those who had no reason to be braided
in moonlight
are bound together.

My friend is back from Cairo.
He is tired in the eyes from all he has seen,
and tired too from drinking whiskey straight
in the little dusty cafés, keeping up with the company.
We drink a little whiskey to join one far midnight
to another, and because my black-haired orphan
is with us. She whose brown eyes
have added a crackling to the night, whose body,
lithe and brown, came somehow to rest
for swift years near that of my brother.

But for a night within the smell of mountains
we are sisters another way, and her glances, black butterflies
of the general soul, join me to one
who is missing, who sleeps like a hive of wild honey,
who sleeps with his sweetness
intact like a blue door sure and firm
in the swift corridors of the night.

He who tries to wrest shards of love from the world
in broad daylight, who loves only a little
at first, then madly. 'Love,
such a run-down subject,' said the ancient poet
of Rio. My orphan smiles and clicks
her whiskey glass to mine.

In Cairo the camels throw the weight of their haunches
onto their knees and raise up. An old man passes through
the café swinging from a chain his brass cylinder embossed
with stars and half-moons. The charred droplets of burnt musk
rain over us, seep through our sleeves onto our skin.
My friend is talking about his Italian motorcycle.
Love, such a run-down subject, especially,
forced as I am, to mix these living creatures
with ghosts, haughty with the axe-edge beauty
of a woman's indifference, with the sleeping lips of that one
who lies even more deeply asleep in me
like a trail of cut flowers from my doorstep to his.

Suddenly the bar is noisy, the music
a raw throb at the base of the brain. We can't talk about love
or anything else in here. Time to put our arms
around each other's waists – my man, my woman, my
unapproachable dream. Time to walk out
into the pungent streets of Cairo with kisses of good night
on a street corner where it is dark and cool enough
for weddings that happen all night long
to the frantic pulse of the tabla. Move back, the men
are dancing, the men are showing their sex in their hips, their
bellies and waists. The rose water is splashing our brows
on this street corner, unappointed as we are, but bound inexactly
by whiskey, loud music, Italian motorcycles, by the unknown
parents of my orphan.

And in the wide silence of each step, the implosive blue rose he
dropped unknowingly into my thigh
keeps alive love's ache, love's incandescent whisper
under the black smell of mountains. And I don't know why
we are together, dear ghosts, or why we have to
part. Only that it is precious and that I love
this run-down subject.

I Don't Know You

And you don't know me.
Out of this the loudest appeal
to harm or advantage.
Don't move. I like this ledge
of loose diamonds waiting to be spilled
into the night. Let's shine awhile
without touching. Sensuality is,
after all, a river that is always waiting.
Let's wait another way. Not for
anything, but because waiting
isn't a part of nature. I don't want
to take a step toward death
in anyone's company, not even
for love's sake.

I like how you know not to speak.
If I could arrange a true moment
to startle us into a right communion,
I would have a small boy come toward us now
with a bowl of rainwater.
It isn't for us. We're as unmysterious
to him as rain falling into
rainwater. He puts his lips to the rim
and drinks, but not without seeing us.

So history is made of unconscious glances
threaded by the unreapable memories
of children. But stay a little longer
unconfessed to me as a kiss
we agree to forswear. I love
this slow carriage, the heavy bellies
of the horses, the harness which
has scraped me down to hide.

And now I know you less
and you will never know me
as one reduced by the casual
or even the half-closed eyelid of desire.
That way is ancient but, like twilight, a sign
of elements overlapped against their wills.

Ours is another luster,
as if a soul had died outside the world
and divided itself in two
in order to prepare the lucid, intricate pleasure
of its welcome.

Yes, let's agree also
not to believe in the soul.

While I Sit in a Sunny Place

Tame love that remembers a birthday
but scorns the every-moment,
how you robbed the pit from the cherry,
that wooden pearl I was carrying
under my tongue. Talisman
of silence wedged between the poet's words
when I say, 'Don't you know
I'm the joyful girl inside
the woman with the forever-melting ghost
on her lips?' If the word 'happy'
has a future it's mine because
I don't exist in the favored shell
of what I'm meagerly given. Isn't
there enough sky? Isn't there
laughter and running? Can't the ardor
of one smiling face make a deer leap,
even when to leap could mean
an alternate calamity?

I have only these hot-cold widow's hands
to touch the world back with.
You know that and it doesn't stop you.
Something sacred, a vast accord between
my ghosted-love and how it could
convey the shadow-selves of some happiest
surrender – was this
what brought you?

Be equal to it then, like a deer that chooses
to leap over a rose. Like a rose with its leaping
above it.

216

The Forest She Was Trying to Say

Tonight I feel compassion for everyone,
those who are pitied, along with those who are kissed.
MARINA TSVETAYEVA

The angel wings of the hemlock
aren't for flying. They are the fragrant arms
of a stately spirit held in the shape
of an unlived moment when the world,
in all its woe and splendor, disappeared.
To visit the sunless core
of the forest is to say to the heart,
which is always a remnant, 'Love as if
you will be answered,' and in that fiction
to force love wide
as the invisible net of bird flight
between the boughs. Here tenderness
has squeezed light to infusion.
Why is love so vengeful and absent
because one diamond kiss
fell out of his mouth with sear
intent against my throat?
Did he mean never to be thought of apart
from love? Angel, those wings
aren't for flying but in defiance
of all that harsh traffic
on the soulless plain. This
is the forest, or at least a small
forever-kneeling wood. And we are adorned
and adored here because we wear the gall
of an impossible love.
Angel, don't look at me like one
cast out and piteous. This is Eden
and the gods are elsewhere. Angel,
we will be thrown out. We will fall
down and be that other wild.

Sea Inside the Sea

How well he knows he must lift out
the desolate Buddha, unfurl the scroll
raked anciently with its dragon's claw
of waiting. Silk banner embossed
with the myriad invigorations of the blood
pulling the tide toward us
until our bodies don't hoard eternity
but are spun through with a darting vehemence,
until the abundant thing made of us spikes free
of even its ripening, that moan of white fingers at a depth
that strips the gears of the soul.

I lick salt of him from under his eyes,
from the side of the face. Prise open each wave
in its rising, in its mouth-to-breast-to-groin.
A velvet motionlessness where the halo
lingers as if between two endless afternoons
in which a round presence, most quiet and
most unquiet, is tended. Because love
has decided and made a place of us.
Has once again asked its boldest question
as an answer.

We are the lucidity of salt, jealous
even of its craving. It follows
its thirst with its neck outstretched
so like the shy deer
who come down from the mountain.
They run their quick tongues
over the wet ribbons of seaweed. But we are so far inside
the body-ness of the body, that the hieroglyphics of their hoofprints
inscribe the many-paired lips of the sea's cave mouth
which, even now, drinks wave onto wave.

We are overspent into awakening like the pinched scent
of aniseed that carries its sex
as a bruising. He lifts himself like an answer
in which love, as it knows not to speak
but is many-chasmed, says, 'Ask me. Ask me
anything.' Again, his palm passes over
the mute belly, passes and repasses.

Her gold and silver rings in a heap
on the headboard. His naked hand. Hers
more naked. The sea turned back nightlong
by the blackened tide of her hair
across no shore.

Kisses from the Inside

He has invented a way of guiding
the blind woman so they can step exactly
together. As she is not led, so is he rapid
and ingenious with me. I am like a house lost
in the woods of Soto
whose upper floors are occupied by gypsies.
They braid red yarn into my hair
and light my shadow with candles to keep me
all in light. He wants me all in light,
she who was stumbling three years
with the dead. He picks my feet up
by their heels in his palm. The more
I want to be high and golden, pitiless and
unformed, the more he tears me back
to earth. He rolls me in the red dust
inside the night. Even his kisses
stroke my unwinding from the inside.
The bees fly off from their honey,
their unspeakable frenzies.
In the hovering noon of our devotional midnights
he flies off, until I am sheer and stolen,
rooted deep in the sea air
            because the tide is everything
                    because the tide is everything
and I have never seen the sea.

A Light that Works Itself into the Mind

If the fish could only half-swim
like an agreement to be half-in-love
the vision of its divine fluidity might hesitate
without comfort, without being consumed. But
it must plunge in freedom-light, luminous and
natural as the language of passersby, yet imprecise
enough to keep a true identity. Light
that is a dwelling or a road that still enters
where someone has fled and forfeited a joy
from that day on. By the open window
she is braiding her hair and thinking what to give
amply, while his flesh unlives itself,
urgent at the rim of her slow unreasoning.
Where has he learned to turn back pleasure
like an almost-summer? And what does it mean,
this something lighter-than-himself
he renews in her like a letter read inside out
because its own listening asks something to be told
away from the very moment of its outward light?

Like a child's freshly kissed face
only the honest heart is free, is able
to return its dazzling to the starry, open land.
Everything he fears to tell her is like an image
that pierces the painter's canvas
from the other side. And it stays on her fingertips
as a spider-climb of heart-constraining wonder
long after his wave to wave
has worn away his mouth, the wet sacramental voice
that had been their most silent body.

If This Love Ends

Someone to follow him? I don't think so.
It is like proposing a second heaven
as if it were attainable because you played
with angels in your childhood and believed
in the wings of their flesh.

A young girl strokes the tight braids
of her hair and thinks she is one memory.
A little eye gleams in moonlight
hoping to be freed of its love of water, of
foggy nights, of wings tangled
in the hair of celestial heads.
I would die again for that girl
who received everything the world suggested
as if each moment were an ascension.

But I have used up my deaths in loving him
as he died. And if this love ends
it will have to go on in me
like a mountain behind a town
when the mountain is made to watch that town
enter flames and smoke
until it at last resembles the essence of love,
that impersonation of his heart's heart
which, one day in the girl's second memory,
became a little eye in moonlight
where he lived in her, imperishable
as anything offered to coexist
with the unreplaceable.

Near, As All That Is Lost

Don't play it like it's love.
It's a memory of love.
                The conductor, FRANCIS TRAVIS, instructing
                the volunteer orchestra, Tokyo, Japan

What are we now, who were two unsynchronized eyelids
lifting the day-into-night world beyond its fictions
of life forever? One eye watched
the other eye in its unbound search for a way back
to a language equal to the dream-washing of our past,
that all-severed pledge each death falsely requires.

I couldn't allow the day-star behind the night-star
until another life leaped over
the beautiful rubble memory hid in me.
Now love is my joy-injured orbit like a bow
drawn by an arched wrist across two strings of a cello
and above this, the listening hand
bending one of the notes as pain-in-transit bends
language to purposes outside meaning.
Only then can it hide its resonance
in new love's shadow-drinking.

Such joining bewitches, and not through harmony,
but through a stretching of memory as we don't know
how to speak its sensations, but must play them out
as bodies, as if the wishfulness of the soul to feel
would come into us, as it comes, as it does come.

And now the shadow takes a step for
us. And I speak into the shadow
its love-name, its most tender body: *Morenito, Morenito.*
So it walks for us and lies down for us and polishes
our one body of light, the one that slides over the earth
like a black platter with the world on its shoulders,
with its feet under our feet.

NOTES

Togetsu Bridge: 'Moon Crossing Bridge' is a translation from the Chinese characters for the Togetso Bridge, which spans the river Oi near Kyōto in the Arashiyama area, known for the many important literary works that celebrate its beauty. In the days of the aristocracy there was a fanciful custom called *Ogi-nagashi* of floating fans down the river from boats.

The mountain area on the Sagano side of the bridge is also known for its many temples and as a retreat area for those wishing to take up lives of solitude. As I walked across the Togetsu Bridge in late November of 1990 with two Japanese friends, it occurred to me that I had literally just walked across the title of my book.

The name of the bridge is said to be an allusion to the moon crossing the night sky.

Cherry Blossoms
Sotoba: A long, narrow wooden tablet set up near a grave, inscribed with a sentence from the Buddhist sacred books, and the name of the deceased; supposed to facilitate the entrance of the soul into paradise.

Un Extraño
In the lexicon of bullfighting, *un extraño* is the sudden deadly lunge a bull can make. In common usage, *extraño* is an adjective meaning strange or odd or foreign. An *adorno* is the kiss or touch a matador sometimes gives the bull as a sign of respect before the kill. *El novillito*: little black bull.

Kisses from the Inside
The woods of Soto are near where Federico García Lorca was raised in Andalucia.

Near, As All That Is Lost
Morenito: little dark one.

NEW POEMS

(1995)

I just want to ride my black horse,
to see where he goes.

On Monday night I dreamed I had a copy of the book and was walking through some woods with it, where I came upon a man, an outlaw-type character, like the wild man in the woods of medieval tradition. When I got closer I saw he was Raymond Carver, and I gave him the book, which he took away with him into a deeper part of the woods. The dream was very vivid, and I remember he was very pleased to have the book, and cherished it; he was roughly dressed but his demeanour was gentle and kind. The woods felt like another place of existence, a kind of Arden, and on waking I felt as though I'd gone there to give him the book.

NEIL ASTLEY
(from a letter)

Urgent Story

When the oracle said, 'If you keep pigeons
you will never lose home,' I kept pigeons.
They flicked their red eyes over me,
a deft trampling
of that humanly proud distance
by which remaining aloof
is its own fullness. I administered
crumbs, broke sky with them like breaking

the lemon-light of the soul's amnesia
for what it wants but will neither take
nor truly let go. How it revived me,
to release them! And at that moment of flight
to disavow the imprint, to tear
their compasses out by the roots of
some green meadow they might fly over
on the way to an immaculate freedom, meadow

in which a woman has taken off
her blouse, then taken off the man's flannel shirt
so their sky-drenched arc
of one, then the other above
each other's eyelids is a branding of daylight,
the interior of its black ambush
in which two joys lame the earth a while
with heat and cloudwork under wing-beats.

Then she was quiet with him. And he
with her. The world hummed
with crickets, with bees nudging the lupins.
It is like that when the earth counts
its riches – noisy with desire
even when desire has strengthened our bodies
and moved us into the soak of harmony.

Her nipples in sunlight have crossed his palm
wind-sweet with savor and the rest
is so knelt before
that when they stand upright
the flight-cloud of my tamed birds shapes an arm
too short for praise. Oracle, my dovecot
is an over and over nearer to myself
when its black eyes are empty.

But by nightfall I am dark
before dark if one bird is missing.

Dove that I lost from not caring enough,
Dove left open by love in a meadow,
Dove commanding me not to know
where it sank into the almost-night – for you
I will learn to play the concertina,
to write poems full of hateful jasmine and
longing, to keep the dead alive, to sicken
at the least separation.
Dove, for whose sake
I will never reach home.

Worth It or Not?

She tried to think of all those
who would suffer from such a step.
Again, the banality of sacrifice.
Again, the wish to have no pity
on oneself. To decide in the full calamity
of a projected 'afterwards'
in which one is trapped on islands of ice
in the river and can't turn
back, but must hop upstream, each gash
of opening black as the water
is black when it looks back and forth,
makeshift as any argument, its neither-nor
enough to make of the most elevated spirit
an ordinary lunatic. In her hasty Cabala

intuitions *were* recollections – meaning
that to love was 'to have loved',
simply an echoed obedience, or perhaps
to fall aware of a perpetual state
in which love reanimates itself by recall
so as to call ahead more latently.
In this 'for certain' blue rose
she had traded her pen
for ice, its vermilion sucking

at embrace, their long journey back to
an admonitory 'alas' in which
the *s* so perfectly extended, yet balanced
its genius, that it revived their truce
by indecision, two swift small caves, alone
as the *o*s in cologne, splashing
the moment alive with two sides
of one sure thing.

Because the Dream Is My Tenderest Arm

absence is a margin of strongholds. I go out
and I go out. Love is sequence and
condition: one of the few winter nights
it doesn't rain, one of the few
snowy mountains that refuses to
avalanche, one of my eternally suspended steps
that leads me, feeds me to the clean patch
of night outside his window
miles from where I lie sleeping.

Heart, he lies there sleeping. Heart, you are
only the shell of a confessed desire
wondering what to do next. The rules for love
in dreams command that all short-lived embryos
shaped by separations be dropped suddenly
onto his chest. Poem, you can die now.
He knows in the caverns of his dream's involuntary
memory that I tried to pass the faint explosion
of these disheveled words over his body's echo.

Poem, put your breath down like a pen that knows
it is well used when the message is love,
when the poem has decayed into its heartbeat
and can be expressed simply as these petals I toss
through the dream's window
all night onto his sleeping face.

Heart, it doesn't matter. We were only sleeping
to let the poem know where to find us.
Now let it rain. Let the avalanche
of hours we've spent apart have their say. Only they
have the power to make these words
bear my heartprint as they fall outside the dream.

Poem, you can die now. I'm going to wake him
with my last petal. Now let it rain.
I want to leave a woman-sized body
outside his window with a dream's ambition:
never, no never to be filled
as this soul was with its body.

But if I speak of the soul,
it is only to use a halo of doubt
to mark the site of a true disappearance.

With Her Words Beside Me

That cry of my friend who doesn't want
another woman to reap all she's sown
in a man. As if by guarding
we could keep love fast or at least safe
until it would grow true. But maybe love
is only a cat that goes where it's warm and
more casually tended, allowed
its come and go. I don't know.

I've lived both sides of guarding
and letting go, watched the lover rush backwards
or forwards to another, or accepted,
then treasured that one sent away
who was my joy and sweet reprieve.

Each time what I gave and took was mine
and not mine, as I am the lost work of footprints
scuffed into utterings overlapped
beyond claim in the dirt before the pay-shack.

Still I bend over her letter as over an abyss
out of which women's voices down the ages
lift to blister the night with ferocious resolve
to love until they are loved, themselves
the unadmitted bounty they could not keep.

From the solitary country of men
perhaps such ardent emissaries were also sent.
Imagine the road was long, the way
treacherous. Imagine, as we do,
that even now some are about to arrive.
Yes, I think so. A reciprocal wind
is blowing. I can smell carnations
out of my childhood, a sweet tearing
at the dialogue of the mysterious and the known.

Always these two insistent voices
and the wounded exceeding of women. Such men
they must be sending us!
Yes, I think so.

Wisdom-Mirror

'Not: who is most beautiful? That's
your usual sycophantic hoax. But who,
my glassy vault, is wisest
of us all?' she asked, fingering
the maggoty, absurd frenzy
that served as her heart. The mirror
tossed a rapier glance, then slumped
shadowy with adoration. 'You, my menace,
my throne,' the mirror hissed, 'of course!'
it added for good measure.
'Convince me,' she said, jutting her chin
like a wedge of ice into the clammy blur.

The mirror turned a tranquil cheek,
pensive as a doorjamb. (Only a fool
would trifle with the cunning of her
hammer. This would take some undoing.)

'Make yourself small as that candle flame
on the mantle,' challenged the mirror.
Once again it was the old power-by-reduction
scheme, the woman saw. Nonetheless,
she had a knack for it.

But just as she'd backed to the farthest
room, through a flicker in the trance – a moth
caught fire and touched off the drapes.
'Save me!' cried the mirror, leaping toward
her pigmied glimmer, its walls
aflame. But the woman stood transfixed, licked
from thigh to waist by the scene – a burning mirror
and, reticent at its center, indestructible,
one glowing woman, shivering with heat,
with pleasurable combustion.

When the Enemy Is Illiterate

You must speak as St Francis more than spoke
to the birds – with your hands out, upturned
to show you mean no harm. And, borrowing
a little wisdom from the trees, receive
everything that comes – strange nestings,
exorbitant winds, blind syllables of lightning,
tormented lovers carving their names
in the rough tablet of your lap.

Thus you will be obedient not to speech alone,
which is only the crude horizon upon which a mighty castle
was put to the torch and consumed
in a paralysis of over-exuberant, yet too solemn light.
Uncontending, you must yield intention so fully
that the template behind speech will sound
like a resplendent gong
above the aggrieved yet expectant face – its
closed radiance as the New Year confetti piles up
on your shoulders.

Finally, make yourself the site of a purposeful failure
to decipher harm in the frenzied economy
of any message. Remember virtue's unspoken strategy –
that we are put on earth as seriously as dreams,
as night and silence. The first star of the year
is always over our shoulders.
Take the splendid never-again path
which allows each clamped beak to divine
its surround of feathers.
Oh glad and fearful signs of bravest welcome.

Your Hair Is Red in Sunlight
(for Mihnea)

'Don't worry, I'll always take care
of you,' he said, as if a promise
had bound him to the instant.

He was twelve when he said it,
yet his delight was an old sensuality
like the craggy thrust of branches
from the apple trees we sat under
at Ciorogirla, escaping the July heat
with his poet mother, Liliana, whose name
I returned to its childhood magic, strange
syllables swelling my mouth unaccountably
to call her *Pusha* after the wild cat
brushing my ankle – all the while
his grandmother caressing us with food
carried from the dark kitchen.

The horse carts slashed through
the narrow, child-choked lanes
of the village – unblinking bravery,
the luminous gait of the horses
beating in apple-light above
the caravan-rumble of cement trucks
heading for Bucharest. He lifted my hair,
then let the curtain slip a veil past his gaze:
'Your hair is red in sunlight,' he whispered,
releasing its urgent recloaking against time.

I heard him from starlight then, a javelin
from the past of the past. Guard me,
my *Pusha*, lean cat of hunger and longing,
from the singe of beauty your child adds to me,
innocent of how isolate, even cruel
such pure love is – otherwise how can I release
in manhood that boy, that woman I echo toward,
as he unsays me to her
fervently like hoofbeats on river stones:
'Your hair is red, reddest in sunlight.'

Liliana
(for Liliana Ursu)

The pressed flowers we gathered
on a hillside in El Greco's Toledo
flutter from my notebook – stilled butterflies
of a moment's joy. What imprint do they leave
in the sling of my lap? Proof that the pressure
of a few days can change everything.
Flowers on which I inscribe this poem,
thickened as it is written with absence and trace
of scent, color – its bruised filament dried
to another tenacity. Memory of your passport photo
taken in Bucharest just after 'the halfway
revolution': 'See how happy I was!' Smiling then
among white oleander, my shutter clicking you safely in
and in. Our vanished steps
on a Spanish road and the flattened echo
of hope: 'I want the photograph on my next book of poems
to be happy. So happy!'

Back in Madrid, a slow sweet wind in the Plaza Mayor.
We smoke stubby Dutch cigars while guitar music
unlatches the night. Bounty then of half-lit shop windows
we pass walking back to the hotel. Suddenly you stop
to stare like a beautiful middle-aged child at shoes, so many
kinds of shoes, take from your pocket
the unsteady penciled outline of your son's foot, the crumpled
map of an island we smooth out for him
to step into, that snow-step of the mind to absence.

234

That night, anticipating goodbye, we rub
each other's feet with oil
as if to touch in advance, and so to preserve,
each future step. And yes, to soothe, to anoint, to dedicate
the holy pressure of the body
where it is heaviest and most tender against the earth.
Our destinations then, two clasped pages
I close these words against – mine to Belfast,
yours to Bucharest.

[Madrid, 14 June 1990]

For Yvonne
(Yvonne McDonagh-Gaffney)

Swept to her shoulders and out of the house –
the boys' sweaters, Granny's cardigan – that way
she had as a girl of borrowing
until we forgot to own. Now we coax her back
like a favorite garment that bears her scent,
laughter unravelling, like water breeze
pensive as a bride. How can she be
so everywhere and gone? Just like her to
store up warmth for us, stretching memory
like a sleeve until we are reshaped
by her absence. Coming upon *her* boat
marooned there on shore at Lough Arrow
is such wistfulness toward life
we know enough to turn it over,
climb in, let her hold us across the water.

To Whom Can I Open My Heart?

I step outside to get a clear view
of this night's first stars, but something
urgent and full of an ancient, inexplicable pain
is aloft in the darkness of the hemlocks.
Again and again it makes its shrill cry of panic
that is a plea and a question.

One bird after dark. What has befallen
its nest, its wing, its sun?
So little to tell. Not even the word 'tomorrow'
is world enough to offer myself
hearing it.

Utterly

My spirit was a bee in those days –
the world one gigantic buzz, drooling
sweetness. Sweet unto bursting.
Love ahead. Love under me.

But most of all, that contrary ecstasy
ricocheting inside – the barren racket
love finally makes on its way to silence.

Utterly – to be destroyed in the kingdom
of flowers. Utterly sodden, sundered
into a blank of peace.
Not to remember outside caress
or tender look.

It's like that against the facelessness
of the heart. No contours. Only
unlivable crimson. Only the clustered braille
of a fearless premonition
fumbling the turned cheek.

No, Not Paradise

When the mouth of the lion unhinges
in paradise, do his teeth gleam
with a frenzied trembling left over
from death, that unripe windowpane
we press our faces against to admire
the roofless serenity of beings at ease
with the perpetual?

Or the woman – whose back might as well
be a mountain in profile for how it wears
its stars without looking up – does she
never weep for love like a bonfire
in that undulating consummation of new days?
And if her thighs are immaculate,
will the moon borrow passion
from the heron's blue lament?
And what of her: Shall I go? Shall I stay?

Rather to feast on the raw heart of a dream
in which our animal souls pare away
an earthly sadness so omnipotent
we startle awake, ungentled
as lake water at midnight
whose stars, even in repose, know
they will never be confirmed.
No, not paradise, but the lion's rich red look.

Birthmark

Water on all sides as invitation to memory,
especially the deeply unspoken – or so I think
when, fishing eight miles out from the Elwha,
Stub begins to tell how his son Jimmy died, shot
like any wild thing on a hillside in Idaho, wearing
fluorescent vest and red hat he'd bought him,
making sure Lyle, Jimmy's friend, wouldn't sight
on the moving elk-man against the hillside.

'They knew where he was,' Stub says. 'Knew
he'd staked out exactly there.'

He's back in that instant of choice a boy had
before his bullet pierces friend, father, mother,
brothers, sisters, then zings fifteen years forward into
this boat so the blood of the fish we've caught
congeals along his right wrist,
and he can lift his son this time
as he couldn't then – laid up in the hospital
with appendicitis, telling his son, 'Sure, take the pickup,'
which benediction reverberates as the shot

before the shot, the one this father wants to
call back, the good father's
permissiveness that strikes his own heart
with regret so profound it can never be
assuaged. 'It's only recently
I could even talk about it,' he says.

The milky blue of years swells out from our boat.
It doesn't matter if the fish bite.
My brother and I let the story's silences gentle
absently until we receive a little more
those held past any clear way of mourning –
because some sorrows *are* the amber
and, unresolved, cast us into water
that is only water. Gaps

in the story then, and the son's best girl
marrying Lyle a year after the death. A child born
to them and hardly a year before
divorce, the girl – someone said – just sorry
for him. My brother then, having heard the story
from Larri Ann, asks about the child. Was it so, did it
have a birthmark where his son was shot?
'I never heard that,' Stub says,
and seems, considering it, near dissolving
like the pale, thin crescent above the mountains
at daybreak, a half-moon trying to dwindle
between glances into a trace, a scar
of moon, passed on. As this is passed on
for its quality of fading not quite out,
like a father's love tempted quietly
into flesh again – though no one has said
whether temple or cheek
took the bullet.

So the wound must shine
outside our bodies. Not to illumine, but to chasten
our witnessing, until it takes the force of omen –
something so ahead of us, as dread
we know at last
there is nothing we could have done for that boy
except what is done for him now in the father.
So we sit with him on water
in the clear morning light, helping the cold thing
come true.

238

Essentials

Five miles into the Strait of Juan de Fuca
fishing for silvers in Ray's boat.
Bright September and we joke between strikes
about the fish-gods, offending them,
no doubt, with snatches of Country Western we sing
so broken-hearted we laugh away each devastating proof
of love gone wrong. I wipe a fish scale
from my sunglasses onto the back of my hand, stare
the flat silver spin of it down the mind – strange
as our hooks dragging plugged herring
through the light-frantic calm
behind the boat. Suddenly

the motor floods out. We're drifting.
My brother cranks it, insistence –
that nearly failed language we've kept
from childhood for times like this,
and the humiliation of rescue.
After a grinding eternity, his nagging at odds
works. We're under way again. Cinched

to my waist by the arms, Ray's
lucky fishing shirt flaps in a breeze
off Canada. Larri Ann pours hot chocolate
from the thermos, remembers aloud her friend
who used to ask her
with aggressive bravado, 'Como esta, sheet-head?'
so 'head' is *had*
and I think of English as a punch-line language
that funnies up its questions. Our lines

are in the water. Our 'sheet-hads'
on no important thing. Morris takes a leak
over the side of the boat: 'Four hundred feet deep
and sandy on the bottom,' he says, zipping up.
Laughter in a boat far from shore and
no such thing as spirits.

Don't Wipe Your Madness Off Me

Don't wipe your madness off me
EURIPIDES

I can use it, the way orgies must have fouled
the sacred into fresh pity – supplication or miracle-seeking –
those ancient days when feasts of raw flesh
and wine-invoked dementia preceded the dialogues.

But he's my brother, the one hard to speak of, whose
raving is an after-work tearing of sacrificial meat.
Fourteen hours driving winch on the docks like our father,
the harbor dying, the last logs shipped in a giddy lunge
of cut and run. He raves when we talk about our mother
whom he refuses to see. 'She's dead as far as I'm concerned,
dead,' he says, in that tone that belongs to reason
as it modulates the decorum of its mania. Lucky him.
I don't believe it. Why is he shouting

in this cramped chapel-of-the-woodstove where we
were children? Lucky him, I don't accept
this American tradition of disposable mothers,
Sons-of-the-Haughty-Order-of-Oblivion.
I come with news of her alive and well, though banished
on the near side of town. Lucky you. I'm going to listen,
to let the rip and tear of injuries, real and imagined, foul
my balancing act between the two of you. I know

first hand those coffined scenes, the uncle who broke
with our father, then wept into his hands near a corpse;
the decrepit aunts three years into silence,
who embraced in the mortuary parking lot.
'She's old,' I say, quietly, 'we won't have her long.'
But her spirit is already too strong for him, too proud. It roars
through his cranium, fuels fresh invective, something
about how cruel she was to our father. He forgets
I was there too. Forty years with a boozer, that life
her only river out from happiness.
Yes, I know.

But his eyes are glazed in the filmy slough
of this unmothered birthing. How stern and unappeasable!
smearing my cheeks with the womb-shine of chaos,
unanswerable pain. Lucky. Lucky. To sit with her.

240

To watch the intricate alchemy of the peace she wrests
from my bewilderment at his wild flailing, as if to say: birth
is like that, gradually shorn of claim, a thankless passport out.
Still she reaches. Still she finds – carries him, her lost one,
in that excess of love which belongs not to her,
but to sorrow itself. Yes, I'll go again. That other miracle.
To be a woman who doesn't love sorrow.

Tawny Equilibrium

To gaze so, with the green caress
of an unrestrained memoir,
holds her face to summer's
involuntary choice of beauty
over use. She can be inquired into,
but, like the sentinel parrots
who guard her by looking away,
it is of no use, in a season of sunlight
to apply an ordinary turn of mind
to the extraordinary. She feasts
on a rosy, unthinkable light, and we
are captive, prolonged by harmony
outside our grasp.

Laughter and Stars

I didn't make present
those days he didn't complain
but I knew he was sick, felt
sick, and a look would pass between us,
a doomed look that nonetheless
carried streamers of light like a comet
scratching light across the tablet of the night sky.
We looked into each other
and like the comfort a small branch is to a bird
on a long migration, we took comfort in
the two-way knowing of that look.

I didn't make present enough
his beautiful will as he went to his room
with the fireplace and heaped the fire up
to match the inner burning of his body's candle,
the cells igniting so fast by then
it kept him awake, pacing him wall to wall
in the cage of his body's luster like a panther
of the will, supple and searching its parameters.
He fed the fire; he wrote
                                poems.

No, I couldn't make present
the tender way he took my body in the night
into his arms, holding his one radiance to me
like a wet match upon which one
dry spot remained and he turned just so and struck himself
against me and there was a blazing up, the way the night
ignites with more than lips and parted legs
when two souls
in their firefly selves
come together asking
to be buried in the no-song-left-but-this
                                dark.

Had I been able to give these things
I might have described his innocent laughter
with a friend and me the night before his death, laughter
at the clumsiness of the body, his body,
with the oxygen tank attached, making sure the tube
was in his mouth. His wanting to go out onto
the deck of the house to see the stars again. The wheelchair
catching on the rug, the oxygen tank
trying to jolt loose, but somehow everything jangling along
out the sliding glass doors, and the sky huge
with a madman's moon, huge as a man's heart on its last
breath-beat so we had to shield ourselves
and turn away to find the
                                stars.

Such a plaintive, farewell hissing
they made, like diamonds imbedded
in the blue-black breast of forever. But then
it was the night before my love's last morning,
and we were together, one body to another, laughter
and stars, laughter and stars.

242

Then he got up, stood up with everything still attached and we
helped him hack open a bright crevasse in the night, to hurl
his heart-beat like the red living fist it was
one more time
out across the sleeping thresholds
of the living.

For Certain Foreign Anthologists of Raymond Carver

Excised – the poem where we stand naked
on a balcony in Zurich overlooking the lake
as if created that instant and fortunate to be
set down an arm's length from each other. Excised –
the hummingbird, your fiery, sensual
emblem for me. Excised – the earwig, uncanny
messenger of the brute in each of us, so
democratically ours we laugh the other side
of guilt into the world's fist coming down on it.
Gone too, your adolescent hound's nose
for women's lingerie in Woolworth's in 1954,
phantom sweetness in the nylon cling of crotch

to palm. They would have you drunk and dissolute
in Sacramento, grim and slipshod in Palo Alto,
the black eel of self-disgust wound forever
to your neck like an amulet. But you had a gift
for tenderness, for laughter
that could unhinge rooms, can still lift
the sere moment of another's pain
because it ignites the kinship of your own.

Down the blank corridors of death your echo is nothing
if not congenial, worn down at the heels by love
like your everyday shoes, so tender without you
not even God could throw them out.
What shorthand biographers of the soul
could usurp such fertility of soil?
Which is love. And able
to quash this lock-jawed, alien scribbling

across the fleshy tablet
of our lives. Yes, as long as one of us
is still above ground, our reconstitution,
the impoverishment of aftermath
will be delayed. Call me tyrant, usurper, despot.
Then, open the book
and read.

Owl-Spirit Dwelling

Especially what matters, this being America
so our absences from the loved place
make it harbor-like while we rummage in the elsewhere.
Without us it ebbs and flows, tidal
but recording too what we would do
and what was done, caressing
that unaccountable corridor leading to the moment after
the bird has flown. To fashion such articulate

waiting is to trace an interior something like a runway
where nothing impedes our taking off, yet
we are sword-hilt sheathed by intention whether at lift-off or
touching down, and we *do* touch
down, do soar. For these are airways bright
with haunting, as when cloud-shadow supposes
along a far ridge, then smudges into tree line until
our looking outward is a hooding above

as from below, an owl's lids, the eye abundant
yet human-sized, capable of simultaneous focus, near
and far, the rooms incredibly light-gathering
and light-concentrating, particularly comblike where
in darkness interlaced with branches
flight is a smooth, soundless muscle our mind causes,
its body opened finally like a bowl speckled
with rainwater. As if the forest had moved in, we too
are speckled, pinged by a multitudinous

sense of homecoming. Like an owl captured in the silo
of its thoughtless concentration, we must turn,
raise or lower the entire head
to take in our surround which yields through
a nictitating membrane over all, translucent and protective
as in a struggle with prey or when
with tremors we hear a voice say: 'Nobody comes here now
but me.' Shaftlike then with remove, a wise sweetness
punctuates, as if a well had been made to stand above earth
and still hold water deeply for dipping into, the sound

of overspill and bucket-clang, gull-flicker 'out there' too
and the light, clothesline playful. And because we are there
when most far off, something of the sea
roars inchoate so we are enfolded
in thought become memory, all-purpose, yet also historic
as in a succession of rooms in a Chekhov story where
the grandfather killed himself in the bedroom and in the dining-room
a man had been flogged to death. Somewhere the languor
of the handsome man 'spoilt by too much love' leads to

a ballroom of elderly ladies dressed like young ones. Domelike
that knowledge at the top of sun-drenched stairs that 'the hour
cometh'. One room then especially and only
for dying. The owl-soul which perches there able to hear
'the footfalls of a beetle in the grass at a distance of
well over 100 yards', its placement asymmetrical as if
it were a second nest, the first having been destroyed or
disturbed. A place of incubation. An echo

of alcoves throughout, admitting continually that step
to the side in order to inhabit or to cherish, though a wing would
call this more habitat than nest – the sounds
to be made here soft and far-carrying, slightly tremulous:
three short notes, a pause, then one longer, concluding note,
until we have drifted down through something, a place
which repeats two distances, until the moon, even that
goes down with it and the word 'solace', only that.

Two bracelets

I wear on my left arm – one
of silver, the other gold.

I am your silver.
You are my gold.
My gold in you.
In me, your silver.

When I slip on my dress
in the morning, when I take it off
in the dark, my gold
clicks against your silver.
I hear it in my farthest
cave. You hear it
wherever you are and pause
as if a wing-shadow
had passed over your heart.

Why is it me? Why is it you?
My gold, my silver – how
can I know? At my wrist
the beaten silver
riding the hammered gold.
It is you. It is me.

I arrange my hair, lift it high
off my neck. My gold
slips over my silver. What
does it know of reasons.
Love is strong enough not to know.

I chop the wood for our fire.
Inside the blow of the axe-edge
the wood breaks open. My arm
forgets its silver, its gold – though,
like a small silver cry
something has carried its gold
into the stricken air, something
is speaking, a sparkling that echoes.

Inscription of light issuing from what
I have given myself in your name,
in your most unspoken
name, the one the world
will pierce with arrows, the one
without answers, the name
I don't know how to call you
except like a woman
so unbound to her love
she puts her body through the hoop of it
every time she reaches or
turns, and the love
is daily and splendid
that she chooses inside his
choosing, that asks him to give over,
that he gives over, and brings out
of their joining – now
silver, now gold.

Why is it me? Why is it you?
My bracelets in their chattering.
Each time they touch
is the right time.
This love, it's an ambush of unison.
My most unspoken, my cloudy silver – gold
unfathomable.

Child Singing

(for Rijl)

Where were we going? Destination fades
in music. The one thing left of that night
in a darkened car – her singing, how it came
from her like breath made audible, yet happened
to her and not for anyone. If the car
had been rolling along with only herself
in the back seat, she would have been singing.

That time dissolved now, swirled
into pure voice, as memory itself effortlessly
allows us to reach altitude, the way
walking alone in mountains
makes songs easy to recall. Those times
the heart lodged inside memory
breaks through the barriers of raw decision
that plague it with fault. In song
the invented continuity falls away
like a hand used alternately to shield,
then bare the eyes in mountain sun.

But her face in darkness,
her braided, golden hair in darkness, wore
our listening so it turned to singing, as it had to.
Rough cargo of forgetfulness, buoyant
as the head of a poppy, we rushed along
with her as down a streambed distant, a mind
having to gentle itself
against its own shadows.
These word-ghosts of witnessing,
to know simply that some things are ideal
and must be left so.

There was singing.
We never reached home.

From Moss-Light to Hopper with Love

Or as a woman fond of wearing hats opined: 'Chic chapeau!'
catching me pensive in the microwave fluorescence
of the pharmacy, buying a pack
of red Trojans, unsure where a certain amour
was heading, but not above precautions. Handy,

a hat under such conditions, to shield the shoe-ward
glance, the muffled smile that hints toward
a bald indiscretion. Being bald yourself,
you would commiserate with the unfurnished apartment
of my eye-to-eye with her, slashed

by a brim of voluptuous gloom where a shadow tranced
my cheekbones. At such moments a hat can make
all the difference, since cat-like, we are creatures invigorated
by notions of dignity. So on film Marie Lloyd
became 'an expressive figure' for the British lower classes,

and Ray's stories tore down more than motorcycles
in rented living rooms across America
to announce the sinking middle and working classes.
An expressive figure, you seem to say, lends dignity
to moments alone in the stairwell, or emboldens our solitude

when love, even at one's elbow, is mostly craving
and window-gazing. If dignity were not precarious, we would be
worth less. 'There goes my dignity,' shrugged the Irish musician
Joe Burke, at O'Toole's one midnight, pulling a drunken mate's foot
out of his accordion. Dazed as I am by hemlock shadow, it

is foreign to encounter the bald intensity of your nearly criminal
sunlight, so white it drives out yellow, the way concrete
in sunlight cousins marble. Daylight, when it is *that* white, is
night's apostasy – as too much loneliness companions itself.
A day with you and I am inwardly shouting: 'I suffer like a door!'

for those women in your paintings who could not even think to shout,
ignored in train cars or offices at night. Their despair wasn't chic,
then or now. On their behalf we must swing pressure to the moment
because the present is, as you insist, clean and tearing enough to
hold back the overhang of future. But how relieved I am!

to be at the fountain's center with *you*. The gush and sparkle,
so silent here – I am buxomly relieved and clumsily
gorgeous, my haunches at a bay mare sway – as if to say
'Take that, Degas!' And what would you make of the starved-down
magazine waifs of my time, these blitzkrieg-of-the-spirit

inhalations? Aren't we as perishingly alive and nose-to-nose
with the unutterable, as fatal to ourselves as they?
Such a long way from the counter
to the purse
with these red Trojans. My hand so below, so at bottom, so
cloud-worn and muted by... solitude trails me off.

You see how easily two puritans slip into the sensual with their
blinds half pulled? A bluish gleam is blushing me
toward you. Could this moment be the calm, desirous darkening
where realism and impressionism overlap? Categories, you see,
like us, my not-so-sweet, are simply errands. To be

fulfilled, yet transitory. And now, my banister, my bald-pated
blank abode, allow me the full gold of this neither-nor in which we
do not meet. This *is* eternity – with my purse snapped shut, its
armory in place. Ah, my glance, my pall-like lids of homage
as I pass you, braced there at the counter above an open book.

Soon, too soon, we will gallop our particles
of 'racing electric impulses' under the viaduct. But first,
that tonic blast of your sunlight, a primitive canon
to the heart. Sultry and expectant, I doff my hat to you, unfurling
Modigliani brows.

Iris Garden in May

(for Georgia Morris (Quigly) Bond)

Seen from the road, a herd of sea horses
spoils towards night under the cherry trees.
Like the mind of their gardener, they swim
sun-shadowed continents in place. Each bloom's
aperture rules an unruly cathedral, love
clowning the sword hilt. Chalice-like
the standard cups after-rain, casques of impulse
eager to shake us wet with vigilante droplets

as we follow her cautiously. Unlike St Teresa
she won't be bribed toward affection
with a sardine. She beheads her Decoration Day
bouquet, prefers hybrids which stretch the rainbow
past color to the under-language of hues and scents.
Heaped with moonlight or plucked suddenly
from the icy spine of winter, they stab into earth
like ardor. If the Rainbow Goddess sent this cavalry

to heaven, the message would be flag-handsome
with new-moon audacity. Ask the gardener if she
has anything to do with their Renaissance velvet,
she answers an imbecile: 'Why sure!'
She admires their not being gradual, sidereal,
digressive as she – for to open all at once
surpasses mere beauty by infinities of welcome.
Where we step, the bulb, chicken-footed, shows

through soil as if to taunt joy with sinister
origins. So long a widow, her litany recognizes
black as congratulatory: *Hello Darkness*, its obsidian
purple-black, *Houdini's* cherry undertones, dark burgundy
of *Black Tornado*, or the falls of *Tabriz* tantalizing
like moths' wings. And there – her tallest black, coveted
by the visitor, never to be cut: *Black Out.*

Index of titles and first lines

(Titles are in italics. The numbers refer to pages.)